Home Sweet Homes

How Bundt Cakes, Bubble Wrap and My Accent Helped Me Survive 9 Moves

Dane Laney Fitzpatrick

By *Diane Laney Fitzpatrick*

ISBN: 1482668017
ISBN-13: 9781482668018
LCCN: 2013904612
CreateSpace Independent Publishing Platform
North Charleston, South Carolina

For Tim, Mike, Jack, and Caroline.
I couldn't imagine this adventure without you.

Introduction

When I got married, I never dreamed I'd turn out to be a moving expert. As a young girl, my grown-up fantasies involved making ruffled curtains for my mod ranch house, wearing hot-pink polyester pants suits, having a platinum blonde beehive bubble, a red Mustang, and three adorable children dressed in pages 925 through 933 of the JCPenney catalog. There were no suitcases in the scenario, no moving vans, and no cardboard boxes. Why move when you're living the 1960s dream?

In Hubbard, Ohio, back then, "kids who moved" ranked right up there with "kids who threw up in school" and "kids who wore casts"—I can still name them all (including the poor kid who did all three). If you had a dad who changed jobs in the middle of your childhood and moved the family, you weren't normal.

My only childhood move was from one end of Hubbard to the other, about a mile down Main Street. Despite my mother's assurances that everything we'd lost or misplaced over fifteen years would be found "when we move," we didn't find squat—not the good scissors, not the thimble, not my brother's Davy Crocket coonskin hat. In fact, during that move, we lost some other things even *more* valuable, if you can imagine that.

My husband's first act of devotion to me was helping me move out of my mom's house into my first apartment. We both had cars about the size of Fisher Price riding toys, so we stuffed them full of my meager belongings and moved them into a furnished apartment above an insurance office. I thought of it as my Mary Tyler Moore apartment, but Coshocton, Ohio, is no Minneapolis. The place had wood paneling on the ceiling and no sink in the bathroom. Mary Richards would have burst into hot, angry tears in Mr. Grant's office.

I call that time of my life The Small Years, when everything was in miniature—my car, my apartment, the number of things I owned, and my paycheck. Tim and I had been on a tiny number of dates, too—four. Helping me *move*? If this wasn't true love and devotion, then it was a freak planetary alignment that had me moving *and* having a boyfriend ripe for helping.

After two years of long-distance dating, Tim helped me relocate from that apartment back to northeastern Ohio, where we got married and began a series of moves from one moldy, malodorous apartment to another. Eventually we upgraded to a duplex apartment and then to our first real house, where we could proudly say we *owned* the mold.

Once we had our first child, Michael, we agreed it was time to leave Youngstown. I saw our move to Cleveland in 1988, when Michael was two years old, as a sign of our adventurous natures, a symbol of independence, a bold undertaking. That was before the movers arrived and broke my Waterford crystal ring tree. From there, we embarked on a journey full of boxes, Bubble Wrap, broken glass, mortgage applications, and new-family welcome packets. Eighteen months after unpacking in Cleveland, we moved to northern Virginia, just outside Washington, DC, and had another baby, Jack. From there we journeyed back to Ohio, this time North Canton, and had a third baby, our daughter Caroline. Then on to suburban Chicago for three years . . . then to southern New Jersey, just outside Philadelphia . . . and then one hundred miles north to northern Jersey, outside New York City . . . and then to Lexington, Kentucky . . . then to South Florida.

By this time, our friends informed us we were now *pencil only* in their address books. We had downright ruined their F pages. Some pieces of our furniture sported six or seven different numbered, color-coded moving tags. We had boxes that hadn't been unpacked for three states. We had stuff that didn't make it, was lost or broken, or, we suspect, had been pocketed by some of the sleazier moving crews, specifically the ones with whiskey breath. (And that was *our* whiskey, by the way.)

Nine moves and counting. Six states. That doesn't count the apartments we flitted in and out of briskly before our first house, moves that didn't involve job changes, homesickness, or wearing pajamas in public.

While we gathered little moss during those years, I did accumulate some experience, as well as a debilitating chip on my shoulder and a well-groomed sense of sarcasm that will melt a small, elderly person.

When writing this book, I browsed some message boards of moving resource websites, and it's pretty grim over there.

"According to many studies, moving to a new house is one of the most stressful experiences in life," one website said, meanly. Then there were some colorful infographics of a stick figure sitting on a block with his perfectly round head in his hands.

"Ten percent of people moving house suffer from hair loss," it said. Moving is more stressful than having a baby, starting a new job, getting married, and meeting new in-laws.

"I'm on Zoloft now," wrote one woman on a message board. That speaks volumes.

If you've ever moved, you may see yourself in my moving follies. I hope you're at the point of your recovery that you can laugh with me at some of our shared antics. If you're about to move, avoid the moving website killjoys and laugh at me instead. But don't get your hopes up. This book is not so much a "how-to" as it is a "how-*not*-to."

Take my advice lightly and preferably with a tumbler of wine. Every move is different because it involves different people and different amounts of baggage—both literal and figurative. But after doing *anything* nine times, I was bound to feel the impact of a full array of possible problems and figure out how to do it better the next time.

So after you've read this book, the tips and the stories that illustrate how I came to them, I hope your next move is a little smoother. Or that you at least keep your sense of humor and indulge in popping the bubble wrap.

I do tend to look back on some parts of my moves with a rosy outlook that is almost fictional. I tend to find the silver lining when I can't find anything else because it got lost in the move. I've heard myself say, "The good news is—" a couple thousand times. "The good news is we don't have to put up with that fat-ass Clipper pooping in our yard anymore." "The good news is I can just say no to the kid selling those local entertainment coupon books and not feel guilty." "The good news is when the plants all die again, I don't have to go buy new ones."

I could sum it up by saying, "It could be worse." I've never moved to a place where I couldn't speak the language, although in Jersey I had to resort to quite a few hand signals (one in particular, but only while driving). I've never moved to a town where I didn't eventually find something that I liked a little bit. And we've always managed to land on our feet with a couple of funny stories to add to the collection. Unfortunately, like a lot of our things, some of them have been mislabeled and lost. We'll find them when we move.

CHAPTER 1

How Do I Spin This When We're Surrounded by Rednecks?

Keeping a Positive Attitude

"Hey, you guys," I'm trying to use my Serious Mom voice, the tone I would have used if I had ever gotten around to giving the kids the facts-of-life talk. "Dad has an interview, and it's in (pause for dramatic effect) Kentucky."

All three of my kids have heard the first part of this monologue before, and it was always that last word they waited for. We have been living in northern New Jersey for three and a half years, and it was almost a record-breaking immobilization for us. They know we're considering moving and are waiting to hear where we're going to land.

I like to set the stage for possible disappointment by getting them ready for something worse. For their birthdays, when I want to prepare them that they're not getting a new iPhone, I tell them I have my eye on a sweet pack of Bic pens for them. Then when they get an Amazon gift card and a DVD, they're reduced to tears of joy and sobs of relief. So I found this little town in Arkansas on the map, one that had a tiny little dot and a font that you had to use a magnifying glass to read, and I told the kids we might be moving there. (I found out later that's where Walmart is headquartered. Who knew?) When you're living in New Jersey and bracing for a cultural shock, Kentucky is an Amazon gift card and a DVD compared to Arkansas.

The kids have different reactions to the word Kentucky. Jack looks at me like I have just told him we're out of Gatorade. To him, this news ranks in at about the same level on his disgust-o-meter. Caroline rolls her eyes. She doesn't believe me. The Arkansas thing has apparently come back to bite me. And Michael bursts out laughing.

"No, really, I'm not making this up," I say. "His interview is in Kentucky."

"Okay, Mom, all right then," Michael says, patting me on the shoulder.

"Fine," I tell them. "If you're not going to believe me, I'm not holding your hand when we end up moving to Kentucky."

Tip #1: Set the tone for your family with cheerful but firm leadership. Think Hitler with packing peanuts.

Attitude is everything here. If you're the mom, you're the leader of your move, and your frame of mind will set the tone for the entire family, including all warm-blooded pets. Don't complain about the packing. Or the fact that you've gotten a painful red mark permanently on the side of your head from being on the phone long enough to find eight new medical specialists with pronounceable names. Don't let your kids hear you threaten to hide your husband's wingtips so he'll miss his job interview.

When your friends respond to your news with, "Oh, I'm so sorry!" (and some of them will, believe me), just paste a smile on your face, try hard not to let it morph into a grimace, and say through your clenched, smiling teeth, "We are excited about this." Say it with some conviction, for crying out loud. And speaking of which, don't let the kids hear you crying out loud.

For me, the hardest part of keeping my new positive attitude was location, location, location. I struggled to keep an open mind about certain cities. When we were moving to the Philadelphia area, all I could think of were the MOVE riots in the '70s. Whenever we talked about moving there, I kept picturing us holed up inside a urine-soaked tenement, which was on fire and full of tear gas, and being shot at by police in riot gear. My kids, in their shabby-chic Abercrombie tees, are peeking out of a broken window behind a dirty bedsheet of a curtain. Not the picture you want to see when you move into a city.

I had equally jaded views of other places that Tim considered for his work and our lives. "What about Phoenix?" *Too much turquoise and silver. I hate the Southwest.* "How about California?" *How about earthquakes?* "Minnesota?" *Wait, I just fell asleep from total and absolute boredom. Minne-what?* "Seattle!" *I'm pretty sure it's all rain and darkness for eleven months out of the year. There's only so much good coffee can make up for.* "How about Detroit?" *Noooooooo!*

The fact is, every city has stereotypes, and it turns out they're rarely true. (Well, except for Minnesota being boring.) I tell my kids, "The suburbs are the suburbs wherever you go," and "People are people everywhere." Translation for those of you whose glass is half empty: "There are rednecks everywhere." Wherever you may move, you're bound to find some nice people, at least one pretty thing, and a Dollar Store.

When I told my kids we were moving to Kentucky, I could feel their pain. The fact is I had already gotten over the denial, the shock, and the grief and was now in Stage Four of Relocation: Talking to Myself Like Someone Off Her Meds.

I'm a firm believer in the power of self-motivation. If you tell yourself enough times that ripping your heart out, wrapping it in beige paper, sticking it in a cardboard box and shipping it across the country is a good thing, you'll begin to believe it's true. You have to say it aloud, though, and you have to say it with some conviction. Over and over . . . and over.

My husband doesn't have a problem trying to stay positive. He loves to move. The heavier the boxes, the more energized he is. The more complicated the mortgage application, the more of a math genius he becomes. He actually enjoys discussing the intricacies of a zoned heat system. When it looks like we may not get the house we want, I become a sample pack of nervous habits. Tim puts his feet up, lights a cigar and, narrowing his eyes like a cage fighter at the start of a match, starts negotiating. He usually chooses to do this on his cell phone in a Red Lobster, far away from me, because I'm no help at all. The Negotiator can't have his wife in the background having a Tourette's syndrome outburst while he's confidently scoffing at a counter offer. Tim loves the mental exhaustion of the whole package—planning, selling, buying, closing, and settling in. He calls it a *recharge*. I call it a quick road to a Xanax weekend.

I've noticed that doctors are very quick to write out prescriptions to take away your stress if you're moving. Like I could successfully organize the relocation of a family of five *without* stress. Stress is the only thing that gets me up in the morning to face that stack of cardboard boxes blocking my bedroom door. And doctors will blame everything that's wrong with you on the fact that you are about to move, are in the middle of a move, or have moved in the past thirty-six months. Tell your doctor you have migraines, are vomiting, and may have had a blackout seizure during your son's piano recital, and he'll say, "Didn't you move two years ago? Do you think maybe it's from that?"

Don't get me wrong. I appreciate the fact that moving ranks high on the life experience stress indicator chart. But you're going to need all the anger, stress, bad temper—every ounce of mean that you've got—to keep that cheerleader smile on your face and lead your family to a victorious move.

Tip #2: Be prepared for the low point, and maybe it won't kick your ass from here until next week.

Every move has a low point. And when I saw low, I mean pretty low. If you've never moved before, or if you've never been in a hospital where there were straps on the bed, you may be in for a shock.

After you've left your friends and the living room drapes you had *finally* talked your husband into agreeing to get, and are in your new home, there will be ups and downs. And then there's the point where you realize all your positive attitude-inducing pep talks were a bunch of bullshit. Your new life sucks.

You must persevere. Hang in there. Touch the bottom of that barrel and push off. Keep repeating the moving maven's mantra: this too shall pass. Pass like a kidney stone the size of a Corn Nut, but pass it shall.

When we moved to south Jersey, my low point came the day I took my daughter to the screening and testing for kindergarten, just several days after we had moved into our house. Buoyed by the fact that I had been able to pull together something decent for us both to wear, I started off in a good mood. Of all my children, Caroline was probably the most independent at that age, and I was confident that she would dazzle the teacher with her ability to recite letters and numbers and pick the correct block.

We sat down in the waiting area, where the other moms were chatting and laughing and talking. I sat quietly, feeling a little bit left out, alongside a woman in a sari, also alone. I was just about to turn to her and start up a conversation when the teacher came out of the testing room with the sari woman's daughter. She stood up and began a loud lecture on how her daughter shouldn't have to waste everyone's time in kindergarten. She had been going to the Montessori school since she was a newborn, and she was now doing fourth grade math. Okay, so Mrs. Sari wasn't a candidate for my new best friend. Then it was Caroline's turn to go with the teacher. She inexplicably turned to me and buried her face in my lap.

I laughed. "Wow, this is really unusual," I told the teacher. "She doesn't usually do this. She's usually not this clingy," I said, pinching Caroline's little fingers to get her to release me. She pinched me back. The teacher was stunned. Apparently this had never happened before in the history of five-year-olds in New Jersey. She started calling other school personnel, pretty much everyone but the custodian, for input on what to do. The whole drama ended with the principal grunting, "Just put on the form 'Won't Leave Mother.'"

"Will that go on her permanent record?" I asked the gathered mass of educators. No one laughed. Caroline and I walked through the dispersing crowd into the testing room, her face still buried in what had been my lap. She was pretty quiet during most of the test, but once I saw she was starting to feel more comfortable, I left the room and returned to the Lonely Loser section of the parents' waiting area. After a while the teacher came out with my daughter.

"She doesn't know any of her letters," the teacher told me.

"Oh, yes, she does," I answered, smiling and shaking my head. "She knows them. She just wasn't telling you."

"No, she doesn't know them. She doesn't even know the letters in her own name."

"Oh, come on," I was starting to get a little bit indignant. Caroline was smiling and had a sucker (or, as I was learning to speak Southjersian, a *lollipop)*. "She knows *C* and *A*. I'm positive she knows *A*," I told the teacher. "There is no way she doesn't know *A*."

"You know," the teacher said, taking off her glasses and setting down Caroline's folder on the table next to us. I was tempted to snatch that permanent record and run like hell. "I know you're new here, and you're really busy, but I think you should read to Caroline."

Read to Caroline? *Read to Caroline?* Didn't she know I had been reading to Caroline since she was in the womb, since I had read to every one of my kids every single night since our first child was born? We had just moved ten large boxes full of children's books, and we had actually worn out a couple of library cards. I couldn't say "eggs and ham" without launching into that obnoxious Seussian rhythm speech pattern for the rest of the sentence. My husband had been a literature major, at least for a couple of semesters, anyway. He's read James Joyce and the Bible. I once spent two weeks obsessively picking apart *The Satanic*

Verses. I know I may not be the perfect mother; God knows I haven't been able to figure out how to get the double-fudgy goodness stain out of the kids' clothes, but one thing I do is read to Caroline! Didn't she know that? *Didn't she know anything at all about us?*"

And there it was—the low point.

No, of course she didn't know anything about us. No one here did. I was living in a place where people thought my kids were stupid—didn't even know *A*, for God's sake—and their mother didn't have the sense to read them books. I wanted to stand up and give her a lecture and show her just who I was. Maybe use some big words. I had to stake my claim here. But I could feel a malaise spread over me. The low point had triumphed. And so I just croaked, "Okay." The teacher went on some more, suggesting some good children's books for me to read to Caroline (books I had memorized while this teacher was struggling through her phys ed requirements in undergrad school) and how to register for the children's story hours at the public library. She handed me a couple of brochures, and I meekly took them. We walked out, Caroline happily skipping beside me.

And I knew that had been my low point, and it could only get better from here.

And of course it did. The rollercoaster we were riding made its way back up another hill, jerking and threatening to make us lose our lunch. And then the ride was over and we wobbled, weak-kneed and sick, on to something else. By the following year, Caroline was using *C* and *A* and lots of other letters in kindergarten, apparently deciding that five is a good age to stop dumbing down, and I became one of the moms chatting and laughing in the Popular Cheerleader/Homecoming Queen section of the parents. I do tend to visit the Lonely Loser section often. Sometimes I rant about our Montessori experience, just to mess with them.

Tip #3: Don't invite drama queens to the farewell party.

Make your goodbyes short and not necessarily all that sweet. It's vital for your survival and your children's future happiness that you cut those ties early and start looking forward.

Keep all going-away parties happy occasions. Push away all morose people, especially children. Some little drama queens and kings will really get off on reminding your children how incredibly *sad* it is that they're moving, how *hard* it's going to be, and how *scary* it will be to walk into the new school on that first day. Tell those kids to go to hell.

"Is there a beach, at least?" one little boy whined at my son. I popped his helium balloon and told him that I heard he was moving, too. To Arkansas.

As you're driving out of your old neighborhood, if you are gulping back sobs, pressing your nose up against the window and drooling on about how much you'll miss the neighborhood *(I always loved that stop sign! Remember that sewer grate?)*, you're going to throw your kids into a state of panic. *If my mom doesn't want to leave, what the heck about me!?*

After putting my family through a Hallmark Original move from Illinois—one in which the neighbors lined up on the street waving slowly, the mailman stopped his truck and saluted us, and somebody's yellow lab followed our car for half a mile—I knew I had to do better. For our next move, one of our friends tried to stage a drama by following us to the car with flowers, a card, and a homemade scrapbook. We jumped in the car, and I hit the gas. Two beeps, a wave, the smell of rubber, and we were out of there. I sent her a nice note afterward.

Once you're in your new town, put all your focus on the new, and start phasing out the old. If in a weak moment you had promised your children you would take them back to visit their old friends *anytime you want, honey!* do so only after they've established some good friends at their new place. I know people who have dragged out the trauma of moving well into the next school year and beyond. The mother kept their old doctors, never switched banks, and signed her son up for his old team when hockey season rolled around.

"We were there so much on weekends anyway," the mother said. She couldn't figure out why her son wasn't making friends and fitting in at his new school.

You may have to create some artificial excitement around the new town. "This is waaaaay better than where we used to live," I told my kids as we were throwing pumpkins into the bed of our pickup truck. We had gotten lost for an hour trying to find a pumpkin patch in central Kentucky for our annual pumpkin-picking extravaganza. By the time we got there, the pumpkins were picked over, the cinnamon doughnuts were stale, and the hot cider was cold.

"Better? Here? Really, how?" they asked.

"Well, for one thing, our state song here starts out, "The sun shines bright on my old Kentucky home, 'tis summer, the people are gay."

The kids start snorting with laughter, forgetting their worries and being left with the vague, unexplained thought that it *is* better here. I'm not above using confusion, treachery, and politically incorrect jokes to see that my children adjust.

CHAPTER 2

Fertile, Mobile, and Hostile
Dealing with a Pregnant Move

Tim and I are sitting in the upstairs bathroom looking at a box of—well, there's no other way to say it—a box of crap that has been thrown together and hastily marked "B RM" which could have meant anything, Bathroom, Bedroom, Boys' Room, Boiler Room, Ballroom, Battering Ram, Basketball Rim. Fittingly, the box contains things you might toss into your purse if you were going on the Let's Make a Deal *show. A box of* lead pencil refills, a scalpel, a Polaroid photo of a stuffed bear sitting on top of a toilet paper dispenser, Lunchable coupons that expired in 1989, and a one-third cup measuring scoop.

"Is this stuff even ours?" my husband asks, picking up a tiny shadowbox with three seashells glued together to look like a crab with googly eyes. "I thought we didn't do beachy cute."

"Oh, yeah, it's ours," I say. "The wallpaper in that bathroom photo of the stuffed bear looks vaguely familiar. Was that from our house in Youngstown? It's ugly enough to have been."

Tim picks up a rubber snake from the bottom of the box and says, "Hey, let's put this in the bathtub and scare the movers!"

It's funny, picturing the mover we had nicknamed Jethro stealthily walking in the bathroom to try to sneak in a box marked X BLTZR and seeing the snake in the bottom of the tub. But not that funny.

Nonetheless I let out a laugh and suddenly feel liquid running down my leg.

"Oh my God, Tim, I think my water just broke!"

My due date is a good three weeks away, but I have a feeling this baby isn't going to be *the schedule-following type. She has already wreaked havoc with everything within a fetal leg's reach of my uterus despite my soothing, sing-song threats to take away her My First Barbie if she doesn't stop.*

"Oh crap," Tim throws the snake across the bathroom, and it lands on the toilet seat. "Get your purse. I'll drive you to the doctor."

"No, you have to stay here with the movers. I'll drive myself into the doctor," I told him. "You stay and keep these guys from spitting all over the front lawn. By the way, what is that stuff? It's like some kind of minty dog shit. Like something a small forest animal would cough—"

"Diane! Focus!"

"Yes," I shake my head and yank down on my maternity top to try to cover the wet spot. "You supervise," I said, "I'll call you if I need to go to the hospital. This town has a hospital, doesn't it?"

I drive to the doctor's office, where I had only been once before, miraculously only getting lost twice, and explain to the receptionist that I think my water broke. Fitzpatrick. F-I-T-Z-Patrick. Diane. No, I don't have an insurance card. It's probably in that box marked FLT STRM that's still on our front lawn.

I get through reception and into an examining room, where they do a litmus test and after an agonizingly long wait in which I read the entire January issue of Working Mother magazine and plan my next career (undercover cop), the doctor finally comes in holding the results.

"What were you doing when this happened?" she asks me.

"Um, I was sitting on the side of the bathtub with my husband, laughing at a rubber snake and a seashell crab," I say. Better to just get myself out there with this doc. Low expectations make for a smoother road ahead.

"Okay, your water didn't break," she says. "You wet your pants."

An hour later, when I pull the van up to our house (only got lost once coming home! Yay!) the front curb is mysteriously lacking a moving truck. Boxes are strewn over the front lawn, and if you didn't know any better you might think we had been the target of a Red Cross air drop, where emergency supplies of toys, VHS tapes, and plastic parsons tables *were desperately needed. The front door is off the hinges and leaning against the front porch askew. It looks like the movers had an emergency smoke break out of state and had to respond stat.*

I find Tim sitting in the living room with a stack of inventory lists and sucking on a cold pizza crust.

"What are you doing back here?" he says. "You're supposed to be calling me to meet you at the hospital."

"I wet my pants. Where are the movers?"

"I sent them home. I got nervous about the baby and everything."

"Oh, for God's sake, Tim! The boxes aren't even all in the house yet and nothing is in the right rooms, and—hey—weren't they supposed to unpack for us?"

"I told them to just hit the road. I can't believe you just wet your pants!"

"Shut up and help me find the box marked JLY FTZ. I think the extra large diapers are in there."

Tip #4: Lower your expectations to somewhere between Rock Bottom and Low on
the Totem Pole. You'll have nowhere to go
but up.

Letting a pregnant woman move is like sending
someone who wears glasses up into space. It's just
not a good idea because it adds too much unpre-
dictability and equipment to an already complex
situation.

It sometimes must be done anyway. If you find
yourself pregnant and moving, you get a reprieve
from all moving rules and regulations. You must
remind everyone with whom you come into contact of this fact. *This is not going to be a smooth
operation*, tell everyone. *So don't get your hopes
up.*

I've done a pregnant move twice. The first time
wasn't too bad. In Cleveland we had a very sympathetic, female real estate agent who convinced
our relocation company that it simply could not
put our house on the market until we had moved
out.

"I just told them that you're in no condition to
be showing a house," she told me.

I liked to think she meant I was too delicate to handle strangers coming to the house, and I might have a spell. I now suspect she meant my bloated, pimply-faced, hormone-ridden self was sure to turn off prospective buyers. No matter how smart of a shopper you are and no matter how ridiculous it seems, you can't help but see the sellers as a walking cosmetics ad:

If we buy this house, we'll look like them.

The Realtors will have no problem telling you to get the kids' drawings off the frig and to ditch the tacky furniture—even remove wallpaper—but they haven't yet crossed the line of telling you to put some makeup on before a showing.

So I was spared selling the house. But I still had to buy one. Our house-hunting trip was supposed to be a dreamy, yuppyish time. Tim was living in an apartment in Georgetown, I was flying in to stay with him for the weekend, and we were going to spend Saturday looking at prospective houses. It was Tim's birthday. He picked me up at the airport, and we went back to his apartment, a really cool efficiency with an interior brick wall and lots of gleaming windows. We got me unpacked and headed outside for a stroll through Georgetown and hopefully to some unbelievably cosmo-metro place for dinner.

It was a beautiful May night in Georgetown. The streets were filled with people wearing hats and other trendy accessories and musicians playing jazz. Even the street people looked hip. I was starting to feel pretty good about the house hunt, and for that matter, the move in general. What a cool place to live! We can come down here on Friday nights, go to a martini bar, and walk around with all the cool people! Heck, we can *be* the cool people!

Then I remembered I was pregnant, and while everyone else looked like they stepped off the runway, I was doing more of a lurch in my tent shirt. Soon, I wasn't feeling very well. At all. I turned to Tim and said, lamely, "Happy Birthday!" And then I leaned into an alley and threw up.

House hunting the next day took a little longer than our Realtor expected. I had to pee and/or rest and/or throw up in every townhouse we looked at, even the ones where an extended family of eighteen was living and operating a medium-sized business out of a three-bedroom end unit with one toilet. We found a house, but I think it may have been because it had the least vile bathroom.

Getting four-year-old Michael and me to Virginia once it came time to move was a feat. I didn't have the physical or mental stability to drive from Ohio to Virginia, and there aren't enough rest stops along the route anyway, so we put our Jeep Wrangler right onto the moving van with the rest of our stuff, and I booked a flight for Michael and me. Tim would set a pattern of moves to come by already being in the new city and missing out on most of the moving day drama. After everything was packed into boxes, our moving crew loaded the truck, with me following them around collecting little things that were left behind the furniture.

This is when I found out that Michael had spent the last year and a half putting tiny toys, office supplies, and sample bottles of shampoo—basically anything smaller than his little fist—behind the furniture, like a squirrel hoarding food for the winter. (And there *was* an acorn among the stuff behind the couch, I swear.) As the movers would take out a piece of furniture, I'd gather up the little pile of treasures and stick them in my big Ambassador purse. By the time our house was empty and it was time to go to the airport, my bag was bulging with the biggest assortment of God-knows-what, that the monogrammed "D" looked like it, too, was pregnant.

Arriving at the airport late, I felt like a cow, a herd of one, lumbering and galloping through the airport to make our flight. We got to security, and I plopped my purse down on the conveyor belt. The security guard watching the TV screen stopped the belt, freezing my purse on the screen.

"Ma'am, do you have a gun in your purse?" I didn't think this would be a good time to say just how much easier this whole move would be if I *did* have a gun at my disposal. I assured her I did not. (But I made a mental note to get a small revolver or at least a slingshot and a bunch of rocks before the next move.)

"Do you have a *toy* gun in your purse?" She had noticed little Michael.

I snorted. He was our firstborn. Everyone knows you don't let your first child play with toy guns.

Although he'll quickly make up for it by biting off the corner of a square piece of cheese and making a .22 out of that.

No toy guns, I told her.

"We're going to have to check," she said.

Checking meant taking that purse and dumping it out on the counter next to the conveyor belt. She turned my purse upside down, and things came pouring out. A little crazy ball bounced away down the concourse and out of sight. She gave the bag a shake, and more things sprinkled out. After a minute, I realized she wasn't even looking at the pile. She was staring at me, trying to figure out what kind of a freak would want to take all this stuff onto an airplane.

In the end, she found the culprit, two Matchbox cars that had been in the bottom of my purse positioned in the shape of an L. She smiled and said I was okay to go. It was much harder to fit all that stuff back into my purse, with only minutes to go before my plane boarded.

"Do you need any shampoo?" I asked her. "Acorns?"

Tip #5: The clock is ticking. Go house hunting before it's too late. This is not something you want to turn over to your husband and his BFFs.

Timing is everything here. If you're pregnant and find you'll be moving, get a new house as quickly as possible. If you wait too long, you'll end up doing some things on your own, such as birthing a baby, and some things not at all, like choosing your own house. So pick one. Any one. Fast. Anything you pick out by closing your eyes, spinning, and pointing will be better than the house your husband and his brother pick out without you.

This was the case during my second pregnant move. We had exactly one free weekend to find a house before my travel restrictions set in. Otherwise I ran the risk of still living in Virginia when I gave birth, alone, because Tim would be living 250 miles north in some cool bachelor apartment with chrome, leather and glass. I could imagine him sipping a martini while I launched into Transition Stage labor breathing. Not fair, and not going to happen.

And then there was the possibility of Tim getting to choose our house without me. In those days before digital cameras, e-mail and Internet listings, I would have been reduced to hearing Tim's descriptions of our new home over a phone line, which would have been about as effective as smoke signals. The thought made me nauseous (although at this point, what didn't?). Military families do it all the time, but those poor women end up with houses with mirrors on the bedroom ceiling and a foosball table nailed to the dining room floor.

I could just hear my conversation with Tim.

"Hey, I found us a great place! Gophers have installed a three-hole putting green in the backyard!"

"Does it have a gas stove or electric?"

"Stove?"

"In the kitchen."

"Kitchen?"

So we had one day to find a house with a real estate agent we found by calling random phone numbers in the area code. His name was Tad, and he was about twenty. The whole thing went badly, starting before we even got started on the five-hour drive from DC to Ohio. Tim was on the phone sucking up to his new boss, while Jack and Michael and I waited by the front door—they picking scabs and their noses and I experimenting with ways to button my winter coat over an enormous stomach that I swear was growing as we waited. An hour later we embarked on a death-defying, all-night drive through a snowstorm for our one-and-only-chance house-hunting weekend with Tad.

After about six hours of listening to me keening while clutching a St. Whatshisname medal with one hand and holding up the dashboard with the other, Tim finally agreed to stop in some town in Pennsylvania, where we found a motel. The room was cold, and we lay huddled in the beds for a few hours, none of us sleeping much, but relieved to at least be off the roads. It was the only time in my life that I pulled a motel bedspread all the way up to my chin, not caring about traces of bodily fluids or bedbugs.

The next morning, before dawn, Tim got out of bed and said, "Come on, you guys, we have to get back on the road if we're going to keep our appointment with Tad. He's got to be done in time for his paper route! Chop, chop!" This Tad was starting to grate on my nerves, and I hadn't even met him yet.

Back on the road, nothing had changed other than more snow had fallen during the night, making it even more impossible to see where the road began and ended. By the time we got to Ohio, Tim and I were so traumatized that neither of us could get behind the wheel of anything that went more than five miles per hour. We convinced Tim's brother, Jim, and his wife, Sheree, to chauffeur us on a daylong house-hunt. Jim reluctantly drove our minivan, with Tad in the front passenger seat, holding inaccurate directions to ugly houses.

We did find a house that day. But it was no big surprise that it was pretty lame. The house backed up to a main road that we didn't think would be an issue until the first time we tried to carry on a patio dinner conversation over the roar of semis and good ol' Ohio boy trucks with no mufflers. The location and accompanying traffic wasn't lost on potential buyers when we tried to sell the house eighteen months later, when we were moving again. Tad didn't get the listing.

Tip #6: You are allowed to add "Just Being Pregnant" to your list of things to do. Pregnancy is optional.

Being pregnant during a move has both disadvantages and more disadvantages. That's double the situations in which you find yourself wishing you were married to someone else, the mother of other kids, and a whole different woman altogether, preferably one that doesn't wet her pants. A pregnant woman in a stable environment is bad enough; one on the move is a blooper reel waiting to happen.

Your list of things to do during a pregnant move will become 3-D and eventually start pulsating into something you'd expect to jump out of some guy's chest in a movie. You'll need some different colored Sharpies to keep it in line.

In addition to the regular people's list, you'll need to remember to pack your vitamins, eat food with some nutritional value, locate bathrooms all along your path, and be sure you're within reach of larger and larger elastic-waisted pants as you go along.

The only bright side is that you may pick up a little more sympathy than normal. You've got to work it, though. Keep one hand on your belly at all times and occasionally rub it like it's a genie lamp. Take at least a full minute to get up from a chair. They'll get the picture.

Tip #7: Try paging Doctor Cuddles McDimples.

You'll need to find a new obstetrician quickly. You won't have time to do any checking on credentials, and you won't know anyone to ask for a recommendation. I suggest you resist the temptation to ask the guy who comes to hook up the water line to your icemaker. I've done it and ended up with an obstetrician who played Yanni on a lavender My First Sony tape player while he examined me.

My new-resident status and deadline doctor searches have had me going to obstetricians with dingy tube socks on the stirrups, a Pakistani who said, "This is your third pregnancy? You're done, now are you not? I tie your tubes! I tie your tubes before you leave the hospital!" and one who was stuck on the idea that I might have gestational diabetes, despite test results to the contrary. He kept claiming that the test results got lost, and I would have to be retested; I teetered on the edge of a glucose coma from taking the test so many times.

Since there really is no formula for choosing a good obstetrician on the fly, I suggest you choose your obstetrician by last name. If it has a root word of anything that elicits memories of the wonderment of childhood (balloon, bear, rainbow, puff, hug, binky) you're probably in good hands.

On your first visit to your new obstetrician, check the quality of the magazines in the waiting room. If the doctor truly has your best interests in mind, his or her office will have more than just a handful of outdated *Parent* magazines waiting with you. If there is even a single copy of *Field and Stream*, get the hell out of there.

C H A P T E R 3

Lose the Ceiling Mirrors and the Cherubs, and We Might Have a Deal

How to Stay Sane and Savvy When Buying and Selling a House

The monotonous Pennsylvania highway I've been driving on for hours suddenly turns into an American autobahn, expanding to eight lanes with commuter cars speeding past me. I can barely see the sign that says "BROAD STREET CENTRAL PHILA," my cue to turn right. I can even barely-er see Tim's car in front of me get off at that exit. Just then a stream of cars comes out of nowhere and merges to my right, blocking my path to the exit. I keep driving straight, hoping only to keep my speed up enough to not get creamed by some guy in a BMW talking on a cell phone. I glance down the exit and see the back of Tim's car. Not even brake lights. Does he even care that I'm in a strange city, I don't know where I'm going, and I'm no longer following him?

This is our house-hunting trip to Philadelphia. I had never been in the City of Brotherly Love, but these BMW-driving, cell-phone-talking brothers, who are seemingly conspiring to keep me from exiting this freeway, are not emitting love vibes of any kind.

I am unfazed. This is going to be a great weekend, damn it. At home in Illinois, I left our three children with my mother-in-law. This weekend in Philadelphia, helping Tim get moved into a temporary apartment and looking for a house for us, is the closest thing to a romantic weekend getaway I've had in a long time. Going out for an actual cocktail without having to give up my maraschino cherry to whoever is in the booster seat next to me . . . Putting my makeup on without help from my daughter, who last time made me look like Joan Crawford off her meds . . . And don't even get me started on the lunches out at TGI Fridays, where the Realtor buys us food. With garnish.

It's okay that I'm lost. I can handle this. I figure I just have to get off the highway, as soon as traffic will allow me, turn right somewhere, turn right again, and start looking for that street where Tim's apartment is. I have an address here somewhere. Forty-five minutes later I have screamed a dissertation on the pros and cons of one-way streets (okay, just cons) to an audience of myself. It turns out that I find the apartment by going in concentric squares, like a maze in an Escher drawing, which leads you to the middle (or a fish or a bird), but only if you squint.

I'm there! The apartment building is on the corner of two busy, important streets, both named after lesser known signers of the Declaration of Independence. I can see the building, but I don't know what to do with this big maroon minivan I'm driving. I pull into what looks like a narrow parking garage entrance around the corner.

A bearded man comes sprinting toward my car, frantically waving his arms and shaking his head.

"No! No! No! No! No! No! You can't park here!" He looks like a football ref racing over to the end zone before anyone gets his hopes up.

I roll down my window and yell out, "I'm not trying to park right here! Isn't this a parking garage? Can't I park in this garage?"

"No! No! Garage is full! Back up! Back up!"

"All right! Jeez!" I'm screaming back at him. "Look buddy, I'm pregnant and—oh wait, no I'm not! Ha!" I quickly gather myself together. Hey! I'm house-hunting, and I'm not pregnant! What else have I got?

"Look, buddy, my husband is living in this building, and I need to park. Where am I supposed to park?"

"Garage is full!" He is still waving his arms. "Back up! Back up right now!"

Backing up right now is impossible. Cars are whizzing by in a blur, and every time I think I see an opening, a car zips around the corner and almost smacks into my rear end. My God, there are a lot of silver BMWs in this town. The parking attendant is no help. He is still standing next to my window. He has stopped waving his arms but has been shaking his head for so long, he's losing his balance.

I finally get backed out, but by this time I am sweating profusely (Am I sure I'm not pregnant?) and I still don't know where I am going to park. I drive around a bunch of one-way streets for a while. Six blocks away I find a sign that says Parking, so I whip the minivan in. It's starting to rain.

After handing my car keys to either a parking lot attendant or a homeless man—I can't be sure but don't really care at this point—I start to unload my stuff. I have a large suitcase, a purse as big as a diaper bag (I am absolutely sure I am not pregnant, though), a medium-sized carry-on bag, and two large paper shopping bags, full of various things for Tim's apartment. I manage to get all these hooked onto shoulders, fingers, and other things on my body that have right angles, and I start walking in the direction of the apart- ment building.

The rain is starting to pick up. After two blocks, one of the shopping bags gets wet enough to rip.

I have to stop and set everything down on the sidewalk and decide what to do. The solution seems to take the ripped bag, wrap it around the contents, and squeeze. I hold it in my armpit like I have it in a headlock while hooking the other bags to my available fingers. My progress along the last few blocks is very slow. By the time I get to the apartment building, I am dripping wet, the second shopping bag is starting to disintegrate, and my fingers feel like they're slowly being amputated by twirled paper. The coup de grâce *is to negotiate a revolving door to the apartment building lobby. Once I enter a tall man sashays up to me, stops, looks at me, and cocks his head.*

"Awww!" *he pouts. He sounds like he has seen a picture of a kitten with powdered sugar on its nose.* "You must be Diane!"

I drop everything in my hands onto the lobby floor. My fingers are still clenched into claws. "Do I know you?"

"Well, your husband came in about an hour ago and told me to watch for you," *he says in a sugary voice.* "He said I should look for a lady who is short, cute, has red hair, and who is really pissed off."

"He said I was cute?"

Tip #8: Pre-nap often and prepare for the most exhausting thing since you ran that half marathon when you were twenty.

The hunt for houses is a strange phenomenon. I can't figure out why it's so physically exhausting to drive to a house, walk into the house, walk through all the rooms, walk out, drive to another house, and so on about eight times. And here's the thing: it's only exhausting for the buyers. The real estate agent can do that day after day after day, wearing heels and a scratchy gold blazer and still be obnoxiously happy.

It may have something to do with the fact that you're in a strange town. You don't know your way around, so even if you're the passenger in your real estate agent's car, it's mental exercise just to see unfamiliar things pass by. As human Americans, we're accustomed to being on vacation when we're in a strange place; if being there involves anything more than unfolding a chaise and ordering an umbrella drink, it's just too much for our brains to handle.

At the end of a particularly exhausting househunt in Illinois, I got on an airplane and broke down into loud sobs—partly because I was afraid to fly and I tended to do a hysteria-like, laugh-cry thing when I flew, and partly because the whole trip had been futile because the house we found, fell in love with, and had to have or so-help-me-I'm-not-moving had been whisked out from under us by a bitchy, blonde real estate agent who lived next door and had already handpicked her new neighbor, and it wasn't us.

So I got on that plane knowing I was going to have to do this all over again in a couple of weeks. How could I possibly find a house that perfect? Perfect in every way—except for the fact that I would probably never get along with my next-door neighbor. But mostly I was crying because I was so tired! Tim, whose seat was inexplicably two rows away from mine ("I don't know how that happened!" he said, puzzled. "Must've been a mix-up!"), kept glancing back surreptitiously, pretending not to notice that those sobs were coming from me.

We had spent all weekend looking at houses with our agents, a man-wife team who took turns assuring us that we were going to find the greatest house in a three-town area. At the end of each house-hunting day, Tim and I would regroup at our hotel room and, using a combination of our high IQs and beer, try to pick through the landfill of house information that had been dumped into our heads.

Every few minutes I'd pick up one of the fliers we had strewn across the bed and say, "Was this the house with the wet bar in the living room? Or was it the one with the gold cherub wallpaper border in the kitchen?"

"No, no. This one had the pink kitchen with the doggy-door. The one with the wet bar is the Swingers' House."

We had found that the easiest way to keep the features of each house attached to its home base was to nickname the houses. On that trip we looked at The Swingers' House, The Smelly House, The Basement House, The Pink House, The Kennel, and The 250 House. Guess which one had a round bed under a mirrored ceiling.

The result of the exhaustion after house hunting is that you just don't care anymore where you live. You start to slip into a state of assurance that life in this house, any house really, wouldn't be all that bad. You find yourself turning to your spouse and saying things like, "You know, do we really need a basement that's dry? I mean, come on, are we afraid of a little water? What, are we gonna melt?"

You start not to notice important details—like there is not enough room for a washer *and* a dryer in the laundry room. There is only one electrical outlet in the bedroom. There is no oven in the kitchen. It's like one of those games where you show a group of children a row of things, have them close their eyes, and then remove one of the items. They have to try to guess which one is missing. Every four-year-old knows that it's not easy to spot what's missing because it's, well, it's *missing*. And spotting a missing red crayon couldn't be harder than spotting a missing garage.

When I got my first apartment out of college, I signed a lease and didn't notice until I moved in two weeks later that there was no sink in the bathroom. The landlord had cleverly put a vanity in that spot, and I think maybe a big potted plant. So it's not like there was a big gaping empty spot there with pipes sticking out of the wall that screamed out, "No Sink Here!" I thought about that every time I brushed my teeth bent over the bathtub.

Tip #9: You're smarter than Spy vs. Spy. Set traps, but don't fall for them.

House sellers are sneaky little buggers who try to convince you that if you buy their house, you will live the life of a person whose kitchen counters are always cleared off, who takes baths surrounded by candlelight, and whose house smells like Ye Olde Country Simmerin' Citrus Potpourri twenty-four hours a day.

And not only are homebuyers chronically tired, we're stupid, too. We fall for all the traps, even though we're setting those very same traps ourselves in the house that we're selling *right at that minute*!

I once walked into a townhouse in Virginia and wanted to buy it because the owners were from South America, and they had all this cool Latin stuff all around. They had handwoven throw pillows on the couch, a beautiful rug, and rustic, carved wooden masks hung on the walls. I'm a basically smart person, and I knew—absolutely no question about it—they were *not* going to leave those masks for me to keep. Nonetheless, there was a little voice inside me that said, "If we live here, we'll be like them." And they were clearly awesome, international types who spoke with accents and drank imported tea. (Boxes and boxes of it, in the cupboard over the sink.) Moreover, I knew that the rug I loved so much was actually hiding a cigarette burn in the carpet. Actually, it was more than a cigarette burn. It looked like someone had hosted a Girl Scout meeting and got carried away with making s'mores. I knew this, yet I didn't care. I just wanted the house so I could go home and take a long nap and then start planning my new life as a Bolivian expat.

Tip #10: Don't listen to advice from anyone under twenty-one. Their sense of taste hasn't fully developed, and you'll end up in something tacky.

Twice we took our children on our house hunts. That's a double-edged sword. On one hand you have extra sets of eyes to help you spot things like the fence next door that has been gnawed to bits by pit bulls and Dobermans. On the other hand, kids tend to get attached to the worst houses on the list and end up crying and threatening to seek therapy for making them move so much if you don't pick the house with the little secret door to nothing.

"But it's a door to nothing," I tell them. "It isn't even something you can use. Believe me, you will never open or close that door. There's nothing behind it."

"But it's such a cool little secret door!" they whine.

When we moved to Kentucky, my daughter fell in love with The Perfect House, nicknamed by her because that's what the seller told us it would be. "This is going to be the perfect house!" our Realtor said on the drive over there. Since when do my kids believe what adults tell them? They're little cynics until you want them to be, and then they fall hook, line, and sinker for a guy in a plaid blazer.

The Perfect House had a player piano—a white, baby-grand, player piano—on full volume in the living room when we walked in, thus earning it a second nickname—Liberace's Ghost's House. Mirrors on the walls, gold filigree on anything filigreeable, and pink everything else. I smelled Crabtree & Evelyn and instinctively knew it had been sprayed from a pink can. The kids' bedrooms were tiny, all with pink walls and pink shag carpeting. The pink master bedroom was as big as our entire first apartment. Besides a king-sized bed and dressers, it comfortably held three pieces of exercise equipment and a Christmas tree. The attached bath had a sunken tub with a crystal chandelier over it.

I was speechless. Plus, the Crabtree & Evelyn was causing me to not breathe through my nose, and talking would have given that away. Caroline wanted that house. Bad.

"I love The Perfect House," she gushed and whined at the same time.

"Caroline, there was not one blade of grass. There was no yard. Where would Gracie go to the bathroom?" Yes, I admit it: I used our dog's fondness for going to the bathroom on grass to get my way. I was that desperate.

"But did you see that little cubby in the basement with all the dolls in it?"

I tried to tell her that the dolls did not convey, but I couldn't help but be sympathetic. I knew how she felt. She had gotten swept up in the real estate rush, where love at first sight is hard to combat. Once you fall in love with the doll cubby or the secret door to nothing, it's hard to fall out of love with the rest of the house. It helps, however, when your dad nips it in the bud by snapping, "We're not buying that piece of crap. Now get psyched for the next one."

The times that we included our children in our search for a new home Tim came up with a selection system where each member of the family got input into the decision. We each got a first, second, and third choice. First choices got three points, second choices two points, and third choices one point. In north Jersey, we sat around a big, round table at a pub and added up our votes. It was tense. I was afraid we'd end up with a house that none of us really liked, but which somehow eked out enough points in a freakish house-voting catastrophe. Math can be like that, I've found. I tried to bribe the kids to vote my way, using whatever was in my notes.

"Remember," I told them before they put pencil to napkin, "the Bad Twin is named that for a reason. Only a mental case would paint woodwork those crazy colors. The Good Twin would be okay for a second choice, but I think you all know how I feel about The Gourmet Kitchen House." I paused here for dramatic effect and to let them really think about how wonderful their lives would be if they had a mother who lived in The Gourmet Kitchen House. "And The Castle is great for Caroline because it has a girly princess suite, but Jack and Michael, you guys are screwed in there."

Tip #11: Charts are your friends at a time like this.

House hunting can be simplified, but only if you design your own fill-in-the-blank form for each house you look at. For my first move, I used the pre-fab sheets given to me by a real estate agent, but they weren't for me. I eventually moved up to a lean, mean, highly customized packet of forms that I had designed and printed out, one for each house. It had blanks for my comments as well as "Pluses" and "Minuses" on each room. It also had giant-lettered reminders to myself, such as "IS THERE A PANTRY?" the result of once buying a house without one and not realizing it until I tried to put away groceries for a family of five into two tiny cupboards that wouldn't fit a single tall cereal box.

Of course, trying to fill in those forms while being led through the house by our Realtor at breakneck speed is another story. At first I tried to be very thorough. I put my packet of forms on a clipboard, which helped make me look like a force to be reckoned with. On one house under "Kitchen" I was noting that the countertops were *Ubatuba* granite, was naming the brand of faucet, and was paying attention to spelling and punctuation.

"Is "trey" ceiling with an *a* or an *e*?" I asked my Realtor.

Before long, however, I was leaving the clipboard in the car and cramming a folded-up form in my pocket, whipping it out and writing on it in the air. My notes look like a dying man's will. On one, under "Family Room," I have written "nce crpee—riff buber" (which I believe means either "nice carpet—rough Berber" or "the niece is creepy—refers to blubber"). Under "Kitchen" I scrawled "yes."

Tip #12: Don't forget about your old house. Remember? The one you still have to sell?

Maybe one reason it's so exhausting looking for a new home is that there's a piece of yourself back in the old town, thinking about how you're going to sell your current house so that you can afford another one. *If we get x-amount for our house, we can afford the first five houses on our tour, but not the last two.* So while you're tallying up crown molding, storage space, and square footage on a prospective house, you're simultaneously figuring out how you can improve on your old house to bring in more bucks to be able to afford that crown molding, storage space, and square footage. It can give you a headache, especially if you're like me, and not very good at story problems.

When we were house hunting in south Jersey, we hadn't had a showing back in Illinois for two weeks. It was getting grim. Tim and I were both getting nervous. But as soon as I left for Philly, my mother-in-law, who was at our house babysitting, started getting calls for showings. She called me at the end of my first day away.

"Well, we've had some activity here," she said, mysteriously.

"That dog *still* has diarrhea?"

"Well, yes, but that's not what I meant. We had four showings today."

"Oh, brother, what did you do with the kids and the dog?" I had advised her to evacuate if we had anyone show up. We had gone through practice drills.

"We went to the river." It sounded like she meant to drown them, which wouldn't have surprised me. Having my kids in the house when you're trying to make the house look like good people live there is difficult. Whenever I would get a call for a showing, I would casually say, "Oh sure, send them right over! Any time! Now is fine!" Then I would hang up the phone and run around the house like a maniac, screaming at the kids to "Clean up! Clean up! Lights on! Lights *on!*"

Grabbing a couple of large garbage bags, I'd fill them with everything that didn't look good—dirty clothes, anything Suave or store-brand, noneducational toys, dirty dishes, homework, the dog dish, and everything on the kitchen counter. And while I was tossing the bags in the van and rounding up the dog, the kids would be getting out more tacky things for display. It was a clear case of sabotage. They didn't want our house to look good. If no one wants to buy it, we'll have to stay here, they reasoned. Either that or they were avoiding what came next—riding around in the van full of hot dog breath and those garbage bags full of crap, with nothing to do while our house was being shown. Sometimes we'd just drive up and down our street, until I realized that we were single-handedly causing high traffic on our street, a definite negative on a buyers' list.

My mother-in-law chose a river walk, but the kids got bored with the same old dead fish and worm smell, so they trudged back to the house dragging some seaweed and river bottom sludge with them. Whereupon they came face to face with the female house looker, who took the opportunity to voice her opinion that we had too many toys. My kids put on their gang-banger faces and assumed a rumble posture around Grandma.

"Make her an offer," my mother-in-law said. "Maybe she'll leave some Power Rangers for you."

The heartbreak of moving is that by the time you fix up your old house to sell, you wonder why you didn't make those improvements for yourself to enjoy. Once you clear off the kitchen counters, touch up the paint, and wipe away all traces that anyone lives there, you think, *Hey, this house isn't so bad after all. Why didn't I do this for myself? I deserve it!*

When we were selling our house in Cleveland, I borrowed my sister Kathy's good sweeper, the one with enough power to suck a Wizard of Oz collectible figurine out from under the bed from three feet away. It had all kinds of attachments, including a pointy one that could get years of dust and grime out of the crack where the woodwork meets the carpet. For the first time since we had moved into the house, it was vacuumed like it was supposed to be.

"Was this carpet always white?" my husband asked when I was finished.

"Yes, apparently. We're going to have to change the listing description."

In the middle of selling a house, your shower won't have any shampoo in it, your dresser will be wiped clear of perfume bottles or hand cream. The laundry room won't have any clothes in it—clean, dirty, wrinkly, or otherwise. You'd think that robots lived here or you had recently been robbed. For some reason, this helps to sell a house.

Homebuyers are like brain-damaged puppies. A homebuyer can look at a kitchen that's too small, a bathroom that doesn't have a shower, and a bedroom that won't fit your bed, but as long as things are neat and tidy, they'll fall in love with the house and pay any price.

When I sell a house, I don't bake cookies so the smell will make buyers feel like they're moving into their nana's house; I don't put candles and chilling champagne by the tub so the buyers will think they're buying Beyonce's house; I just empty the house of all clutter and anything I bought at Walmart and hope the buyers will think they're moving into a cool person's house.

Open houses are particularly hard when you're selling a house. In the Northeast, real estate open houses are four to five hours long. During one particularly long Sunday open house in north Jersey, we found ourselves in the van with the dog (and as always, those damn bags) and had already gone to lunch, dropped off library books, and returned movies to Blockbuster, using up only the first forty-five minutes. Michael sneaked back into the house to pick up his laptop and a DVD, and we went to the park and watched *Anchorman*. Every half hour we'd pause the movie, I'd turn on the engine, heat up the car, and try to unsteam the windows while one of the kids would walk the dog for a little bit. At the end of the open house, we drove back to the house, only to find cars still in our driveway.

We went inside anyway. There was no way I was going to stay in that car one more minute. We shlupped in, all carrying at least one garbage bag and our movie gear. Our Realtor introduced us to a polite, smiling couple who had come to see the house. We exchanged pleasantries, and they pretended not to notice Jack putting dirty dishes back in the sink and a toaster and coffee maker back onto the counter. They left and our Realtor was starting to put on her coat when I said, "Hey, there's still another car in the driveway." Sure enough, one couple was still in our basement. I still am not sure what they were doing down there, but whatever it was, they were doing it very quietly. I think they may have been hiding down there, hoping we wouldn't notice, to jump out later, saying, "Aha! You live like pigs! We knew it!"

By my ninth move, you would have thought I'd be better at the house showings. But, no, I still had more lessons to learn. Our Kentucky house was on the market, and I knew as of 10:00 p.m. the night before that I was going to have a showing at noon. I figured I'd spend the morning getting the house ready, but we were just coming off an Easter high, where I'd had company and lots of food high in fat, sugar, and egg yolks. I was in a post-Easter malaise that can only come from having given up sweets, alcohol, and Cheez-Its for Lent. Also I had a thin layer of Easter grass covering the entire first floor, candy that wouldn't fit anywhere, and too many leaves in the dining room table. So it took me a little longer to clean up than I expected.

Time began to run out on me. I found myself running through the house with a vacuum hose in one hand, a lawn-and-leaf bag in the other, and a bottle of Windex hooked to my Mom Jeans waistband, paper towels scrunched into my pocket. Fifteen minutes to go, and I opened the oven to discover a broiler pan from the salmon I made for Easter dinner, which I had forgotten about. The smell of fish poured out of the oven into the house. I grabbed the pan and threw it in the car, along with the garbage bag full of Easter candy, some eggs, a week's worth of mail, and some dishes that had to be returned to other people. Back in the house, I did a quick Olympic torch trot through the downstairs with a spray can of Lysol. Back to the car with Grace the dog, her dish, my purse, an extra phone I couldn't find a dock for, some throw rugs, and the teakettle. That's when I saw the half pan of butterscotch pudding dessert in the wintertime second refrigerator, otherwise known as the garage. Into the front seat it goes, one level above the fish-encrusted broiler pan.

That's how Grace and I spent the next two hours. I took her on a walk and then ran some errands, being careful not to be gone too long. It was only going to be a matter of time before Grace discovered that the fish and whipped cream smell was coming from the front seat. We had to spend the last half hour around the corner from our house, with me peering between two trees to see the house-lookers' car so I would know when to go back home. The pudding started looking sooo good . . . but I didn't have a fork . . . .What was I supposed to do? Heck yes, I ate the butterscotch pudding dessert with my hands. It doesn't count if you're moving, right?

As horrific as these scenarios sound, it's still better to be gone from the house when it's being shown. Staying can be worse. Selling and buying a house is very personal, and meeting the people involved is awkward and embarrassing in even the best-case scenario. During one showing when we were just too afraid of the boredom to leave, a six-year-old girl walked up to my son in the kitchen and said, "Can I have some of those Funyuns? Do you watch *Sex in the City?*" He wasn't sure what to say, but had a vague notion to give her the right answer. Was she the customer or were we? It's a tough relationship. You're best off being invisible and anonymous.

One woman told me when their house was for sale, she found out that her nine-year-old daughter had been following people around the house showing them the spots on the carpet where the dog had thrown up. When the mother solved that problem by taking her daughter out during the showings, the daughter resorted to hanging up a sign on her bedroom door that said, "Get Out + Stay Out! Don't Buy This House! We Hate You!" My children have never done that, at least not that

I know of. To be safe, your best bet is to hide the markers and construction paper.

I'll Make You a Bundt Cake If You Say Nice Things About My House

Impressing Your Realtors, Inspectors, Appraisers, and Other Relo Peeps

I am so ready. After days of cleaning, repairing, clearing out, and reorganizing, I have turned my house into the well-oiled machine it isn't. The inspector is coming! The inspector is coming!

The inspector is an older guy, probably retired and doing this for a little extra income. His inspection will determine what my husband's company

will offer us to take our house off our hands, giving us a free pass on selling it ourselves. I would do almost anything that this man's heart could take to get a good inspection report out of him. After I spruced up the house, I put on deodorant and some blush. That's how desperate I am to impress him.

He arrives, and I walk him through the whole house, downstairs, upstairs, I open the pull-down attic door and let him take a peek. Then we go into the basement.

"Here's the unfinished storage area," I say, leading him through a door. He looks around and jots some things down on his clipboard. I am standing in the center of the room when I hear something behind me. A little scratching sound, like something is being dragged across the cement.

I turn and look behind me, and there, near the workbench but making its way into the center of the room, is a mouse, his head stuck in the business end of a mousetrap. His rear end is off the side edge of the wooden pallet, and his feet are going a mile a minute, scratching at the floor. The foot-scratch has put him into a circular movement, so he is spinning around in a spiral, like the marks you make when you're testing out a pen. He must be getting dizzy as hell. Although with his head stuck in a mousetrap, motion sickness is probably the least of his problems.

Where did this thing come from? I thought the mouse chapter of my life was over. Mice were my nemesis about a year earlier, when the whole field mouse community got word that they should make their way through the corn field and into the house at 33 Byron Drive, a nice warm place, where there are lots of newspapers to shred in the basement and a whole kitchen drawer full of birthday candles in various colors, good for hours of chewing enjoyment. For a few months that year, I set probably twenty-five traps and caught twenty-five mice. Very few in the food cupboards, but a lot in the birthday candle drawer and oddly in the dishtowel/pot holder drawer. (Were they cold? Were they looking for blankets?) And there were lots of mice in the basement, where they found a palatable stash of the kids' kindergarten drawings, seven years' worth of financial receipts, and our marriage license.

We had so many mice that we once found one dead, lying in the middle of the basement floor with no signs of foul play, although we stopped short of asking for a coroner's inquest.

"Maybe he died of old age," Michael said, kneeling over the body, looking closely. "I think we're running a nursing home for mice."

Unfortunately, that was the only mouse that went quietly. For a while I experimented with different kinds of traps. The thought of breaking their little necks bothered me, so I got a couple of those sticky traps that hold them to a board covered with some yellow stuff that is absolutely the stickiest substance on the planet. (Note: If after reading this you still feel you should try these traps, do not—I repeat do not under any circumstances—test them out by putting your finger directly onto the sticky substance. It causes more problems than getting your finger snapped in a regular mousetrap.) I set the first trap in the dishtowel/pot holder drawer in the kitchen.

The next morning I opened the drawer to find the answer to my question How Does This Sticky Trap Kill the Mice? The answer is, The trap doesn't kill them. They kill themselves by trying to chew off the body part that is stuck to the trap, in this case the entire lower half of the mouse. By the evidence, I can also assume that there is a lot of thrashing and throwing of limbs involved, as well as some stomach upset, projectile vomiting, and explosive diarrhea. The ensuing mess was enough to make me want to move away and start over with all new stuff. In actuality I had to start over with all new dishtowels and potholders.

I can't explain why I set a second sticky trap, but I did, in the birthday candle drawer. The next morning I opened the drawer very, very, very slowly, afraid of what I would find. What I found was no blood. No guts. No mouse. No mousetrap.

"What do you mean there was no mousetrap?" my sister Pam asked me when I told her.

"It was gone. The whole mousetrap was gone."

"Are you sure that Tim or one of the kids didn't take it out?"

"God no," I told her. "I set these traps late at night, after everyone's in bed, and I check on them in the morning before anyone else is up. Besides, no one in our family will open drawers in the kitchen anymore."

"What you need to do," Pam said matter-of-factly, "is set three more sticky traps for his other three feet, because you have a mouse walking around your house wearing one big sandal."

I couldn't figure out how the mouse got out of the drawer wearing that thing. There had to have been a rescue by his buddies, probably involving lighters, garbage bag twisties, and a ball of string, all things kept in the next drawer down. This was getting serious, and I couldn't let these little rodents conspire against me. So I set a third trap, back in the dishtowel/pot holder drawer, which now contained a single old rag, a token decoy.

The next morning, I opened the drawer (I now was getting very good at opening drawers so slowly my coffee got cold in the process), and there was the mousetrap, and there was the mouse. There had been no chewing and thrashing and there were no signs of a rescue attempt. But he was still alive. He was lying there on his side, all peaceful-like, his little eyes closed, and his chest pumping up and down with his breath. This was bad. Very, very bad. I wasn't about to touch the trap, afraid that the movement would revive him and he would lash out at my finger, and if I slipped, and my finger ended up on that sticky stuff with a living mouse . . . oh, let's not go there.

So I closed the drawer and stuck a Post It on the outside that said, "DO NOT OPEN. MOUSE INSIDE." It took three days for the mouse to die, with all five of us occasionally opening the drawer to check on his progress and timing his chest movements.

That was the end of my experiment with other kinds of traps. Breaking their necks was the clear winner. So I set more neck-breaker traps in all the hot spots, including all around the basement. Then one day, the mouse grapevine must have gotten word to vacate 33 Byron Drive. Maybe the guy with the sandal finally made it back to the field to report the horrors. In any event, we never had another mouse in the house for the rest of the year.

Which is why I am so surprised to see this thing spinning around on my basement floor, like a living, self-propelled Spirograph. I apparently had forgotten I had a trap still set under the workbench and here was this little renegade who hadn't gotten the word to stay out of 33 Byron and head on over to the basement of 31 Byron, where there was a fabulous feast of two life-size fabric Christmas caroler dolls.

Anyone who has used the phrase, "As quiet as a mouse" clearly was not talking about one whose head is stuck in a trap. The scraping and the scratching. I quickly turn back around and see that the inspector is still writing. He apparently is hard of hearing. I cannot let him see this mouse. I don't have time to think about whether or not the presence of mice even makes it into an inspection report, but something tells me it isn't a good thing. I start talking loudly and shuffling and stamping my feet, while blocking his view of the mouse behind me. He must think I have to go to the bathroom. I yell, "I need to show you the refrigerator that's going to stay! It's right over there!" I point to an area around the corner. He gives me a funny look and walks over to the refrigerator. As soon as he is out of sight, I grab an empty cardboard box and turn it over on the mouse. He continues to spin, and when he careens into the side of the box, it shifts a little *bit, but for the most part I figure I have this guy contained.*

As soon as I get the inspector out the front door, I run back down to the basement. There is still some spinning, although, is it my imagination or is it getting slower and less enthusiastic? Occasionally he would spin into the side of the box, but then spin back away. It's muffled anyway. Knowing I can't deal with live mice, I slap on a Post It that says, "DO NOT LIFT UP. MOUSE INSIDE" and go upstairs. When their heads are stuck in a trap, it only takes about twenty-four hours for them to die.

Tip #13: Make your house look nice for the professionals, but don't go all OCD over it.

When you're getting ready to sell your house, you'll hear a lot of nonsense from experts who throw all this advice at you on how to make your house more desirable. Light candles around the bathtub, set the dining room table for a dinner party, bake cookies and swish the smell around the house, get a new stove, kill the mice, blah, blah, blah.

They'll tell you to take half of your junk out of all your closets and cabinets, so a buyer will think there's almost *too much* storage space. You'll also be encouraged to throw away that George Foreman grill that hasn't had the grease scraped off of it in two years, and fix everything that's broken. In some real estate markets, stagers will come in and put your tacky stuff in storage and replace it with Pottery Barn furniture and expensive prints. The danger in doing this is that your house will then be so perfect, you won't want to move.

When my sister Reenie sold a house in Palo Alto, California—a real estate market where an extra Glade Plug-in can get you another $200,000— she was told to store virtually all of her furniture and rent new stuff, as well as get new carpeting and replace all the appliances. What she ended up selling was a different house altogether. She was tempted to buy it off of herself, it was so nice.

There's something about showing your house to inspectors that makes you wish you had been a more shallow but cleaner, neater person. You think about all that time you spent reading Dickens and watching PBS and wish you had spent that time Swiffering. You get an instant view of your life through the eyes of a person who will brazenly open the cabinet under your sink without batting an eye. I mean, really, how nice can the inspector's own house be? I think some of these guys are jealous and try to make you feel bad about your nice house. I try to make myself feel better by picturing him off duty, on a threadbare couch behind a rusty TV tray. There's old, faded, flowery wallpaper on the walls and a smell of warm mayonnaise in the air.

I had one inspector comment that I had obviously "never learned how to pull a drawer." I wasn't even sure what that meant, but I looked it up later and found that some people—get this—a couple times a year pull out their drawers and clean up all the little crumbs and pieces of crud that fall down there behind them. *Behind the actual drawers!* Why not lift up the house and dust the foundation while you're at it? Unless you're looking for change or that lost thumb drive, I can't imagine wanting to clean inside the bowels of my house.

Yet when you're selling a house, the inspectors, appraisers, and real estate agents are the first line of incoming enemy troops. You have to convince them that your house is spotless, critter-free, perfect, better than new! Ideal for families! A fabulous gourmet kitchen! A gorgeous home! You have to sell that to them, before you and they together can conspire to convince potential buyers that it's true.

Here's the conflict in house sales: You want everyone to think your house is great, but if it's that great, why aren't you keeping it? It's like you're saying, "Hey, take this house! It's great! I mean, we certainly don't want it, but it'll be fine for you!"

Tip # 14: Keep a respectful distance from these people. No matter what they say, they are not your real friends.

That group of real estate people and their cronies start out as strangers but in very short order become people you desperately want to impress. When you're making a corporate relocation, if your employer is at all involved in your move, you have extra inspections and appraisals, so that some HR guy in your company will know intimate details about the house they're helping you sell.

In Illinois, we had an appraiser come in and assess how much the relo company should pay us for our house, should we be unable to sell it on our own. This woman was so sweet and unassuming, kind of a schoolmarm type with glasses and her hair in a bun. She became my best friend while I was showing her my *Gorgeous interior!* Afterward we sat at the table in my *Enormous eating area!* in my *Cozy kitchen!* and had coffee and a bundt cake I made from scratch. She seemed so nice. We chatted about our children, and she told me something embarrassing about her husband. I was starting to think we might stay in touch after she was gone. We're talking *friends*, here. A few days later Tim got her report at work.

"You're not going to like this," Tim told me on the phone. He was holding the report, he said. That sounded ominous.

"What! Tell me!"

"I'm not going to read it to you. You'll feel really bad." Then he immediately read it to me.

I couldn't believe it. That Plain Jane had not one nice thing to say about my house! I stopped listening right after Tim read the part about the kitchen, where the wallpaper was apparently "not neutral enough."

"That *hag!*" I snarled. "I gave her *cake!*"

Corporate relocations give you the added pleasure of working with relo specialists, people who are supposed to help guide you through the quagmire of tasks facing you. They help you find a real estate agent, schedule inspections, remind you about utility shut-offs and turn-ons, and call you every few days just to speak to you in a cheerful, pleasant voice. It's all designed to have a calming effect; however, it's actually just another reason to answer the phone again.

Relo specialists are also in charge of sending you big stacks of papers that need to be notarized, each page with specific and unique requirements on exactly how the notary is supposed to sign and stamp, and how you and your husband are to sign. If these are not done correctly, Western Civilization as we know it will cease. If the notary makes a mistake, there are no other copies that can ever be made until the end of time. Worse, you'll get yelled at if you don't do this right.

Heading to the bank in north Jersey with the forms, in a briefcase handcuffed to my wrist, I had butterflies in my stomach. *What if this goes badly?* And of course it did. The notary was almost through the stack of papers when she looked at one page and drew up her hands and backed up her rolling chair. I thought maybe there was a little bit of anthrax on the paper.

"I can't do this one," she said, still not touching the paper, just staring at it. "This one has spaces for both you and your husband to sign, and the part where I have to put my name says I have witnessed the signatures of both of you. You're both not here, so I can't say I witnessed both signatures."

We had gone over this type of screw-up in the pre-signing practice drill prior to our meeting. I had explained to Ms. Integrity that I was going to do my notary thing and then overnight the whole package, handcuffs and all, to Tim, who was already in Kentucky and who would then do his half of the notary thing. It was the only way to get the papers notarized since we would not be physically in the same state until the actual move. And if we were going to be together sometime before then, it certainly wasn't going to be in a bank assistant manager's office, if you get my drift.

"But the other papers have spaces for Tim's signature, too," I whined, "and you put your signature and squeezy-embossing-thingy on those." I was terrified that the butterflies were going to fly up through my mouth.

"But the wording on this one . . . ," she said, slowly shaking her head and exhaling dramatically.

I was in a panic. I left the bank with that one stinking line left blank and spent the next hour driving around Sussex County trying to find a notary whose honor would be compromised for the right price. I had fifteen dollars and some change in my purse, and I was prepared to use it. Surely there was somebody out there who had taken the notary pledge but who had since become a crack addict or had a gambling problem. Life couldn't be 100 percent smooth sailing just because you took an adult ed course at the vocational school.

I eventually found some back-alley notary, between a Laundromat and an adult bookstore in the next county, in an office that smelled like onions and Vitalis. He said he liked my driver's license picture. I smiled awkwardly. I signed. He stamped. And I gave him $15.68 and crossed another item off my moving list.

Tip #15: With your real estate agent, be yourself, only bitchier.

Your relationship with your real estate agent is a precarious thing. Don't let him bully you, and don't give up any control, especially early on. Asking nicely will get you nowhere. On the other hand, being psycho-tearful or patronizingly demanding will anger him and make him restless. Your best bet is to let your agent see a bullwhip hanging in your guest closet on his first visit to your home. This will prove you're a force to be reckoned with.

We've worked with just about every type of real estate agent: From the super-efficient females with manicures and power helmets who are on one long series of cell phone calls throughout the whole process, to my agreeable brother-in-law Bob, who let us call all the shots and who did all the hard work for us, to my other brother-in-law Jim, who is such a natural-born salesman that he was about $17 away from talking someone into selling us a house on which they already had a full-price cash offer.

The best agent we ever had was Helen in south Jersey. We were the talk of the neighborhood the day Helen pulled up in front of our house and took a sign out of the trunk of her Mercedes and pushed it into our front lawn.

"I'm Gorgeous Inside!" it said.

Tim wanted to take a picture of me standing next to it, because I *am* gorgeous inside, or so he claimed. I was suspicious and refused to pose. One of our neighbors asked if he could have the sign when we were done. There was some prank involved, I'm sure. I don't know if the sign had anything to do with it, but we had multiple offers within days. Helen's motto apparently was "Whatever It Takes."

The best buyers' agents are the ones who stroke you into thinking that the house you're about to buy is just right. Because you need to feel good about this, and that's part of their job. Carol, the agent helping us find a house in suburban Washington, knew we'd be in zombie-like sticker shock moving from Cleveland (city motto: Lowest Cost of Living Nationwide Except for Camden, New Jersey) to northern Virginia (motto: Some of our Sardine Cans Have Walk-Outs).

Before our house-hunting trip there, Carol mailed us a packet of listings to look over, just to get an idea of how far down we were going to have to drop on the quality-of-life ladder. We eagerly waited for the package to be delivered, and when it came we tore it open. Carol had attached a note that said, "Sit down before you look at these prices and descriptions." She had scotch-taped four Extra Strength Tylenols to the paper. And she had kindly included a regional map so we could see that the only decent houses we could afford were a good sixty miles from Tim's job.

So we went house-hunting in northern Virginia, prepared for our next reality—moving from a single-family home to a tiny townhouse. From a low-crime bedroom community in the Midwest to a place where drive-by shootings were happening just blocks from the Capitol building. From a low mortgage payment to one that gave me acid reflux. From a big backyard with a gazebo to one that you could mow with a weed whacker.

Carol was so nice to prepare us, but she had a little mean streak. For the three days that we looked at townhouses, she had us meet her at her house, a big, brick colonial with pillars and a circular driveway in ritzy McLean. Apparently the real-estate career was working out pretty well for

Carol. We'd start out the morning in her bright and cheery kitchen with the stainless steel appliances and a view of rose bushes. She would offer me some Dole Pineapple Mango juice in a crystal glass, and I would gaze longingly at the black and white tile foyer floor and the posh drapes. I asked to use the bathroom and couldn't keep my hands off the walls, which were faux painted to look like suede.

Then we'd go see the houses Tim and I could afford. In one townhouse, the window shades in every single room were covered with the same blue-flowered contact paper. Another townhouse had a bathroom that had wallpaper in a brown contemporary swishy design that looked like a two-year-old had gotten creative with a ladder and a dirty diaper. Carol remained cheerful throughout and why wouldn't she be? At the end of the day, she was going back to her dream house and leaving this slum behind.

Some real estate agents go above and beyond their pledge, as they should. They have been big show-offs, and you've been through a trauma. Take their housewarming gifts, accept their invitations, and take them up on their offers to "call me anytime." What they mean by "anytime" is "when you're ready to sell your house again and can bring me some more business," but who cares?

I called our agent, Bob, two days after our move to Illinois because he was the only person I knew west of the Indiana state line, and our water was out. There was a water leak in the basement, so Tim had gone down there, shut off the water to the entire house, then walked outside, got into his car, drove to the airport, and flew to Cleveland on a business trip. I was probably still standing dumb-struck in the basement when his plane touched down. I had laundry to do, dishes to wash, Tang to mix up, and I didn't know a single thing about who to call to fix this problem. I had only met four people there, and none of them was handy, let alone certified plumbers. So I called Bob.

"Are you ready to sell already?" he asked. I promised him that I would keep him in mind when we were ready, so he called a plumber for me.

Some of our past real estate agents still send us Christmas cards. We follow their careers by occa-sionally looking up their current listings online and watching for their Silver/Gold/Bronze/Pewter/ Tin Foil/Million Dollar sales achievements. I'm sure some of our varied relocation professionals remember us as a wacky family, me with my lists and nicknames and Tim's ability to turn a house purchase into an Olympic sport. (He high-fives everyone at the table at the end of closing.) We're well aware that despite the cards, gifts, and air kisses, we're just another client. But I believe them when they say it's been a pleasure working with us. I think we were good for some entertainment.

CHAPTER 5

Boxes, Boxes Everywhere, But Not a Drop of Scotch to Drink

How to Cope on Moving Day Using Whatever Hasn't Been Packed Yet

New Circle Road. What a great idea. You take a city like Lexington, Kentucky, and you put a circular road around it, part freeway and part commercial zone. And then you make all the other major roads like spokes of a wheel, heading out in all directions. Follow any of those roads in, and you end up at Starbucks on

Main Street downtown. *Follow the roads out, and you get to a different suburb. Not bad. And it's especially nice for newcomers. If you're lost, just get on the circle and get off at the appropriate wheel spoke. Or if you miss your exit, keep going and eventually you'll end up back around again.*

I am driving on New Circle, marveling at the concept, and glad to be anywhere outside the house. It is Moving-In Day, and I have volunteered to leave to sign papers at the insurance office on the other end of town. Our moving crew had arrived a couple hours earlier, the pads are taped to the floor, and the brown paper is on the carpet. Doors have been taken off their hinges, cigarettes are being put out, and stuff is starting to make its way from the truck.

"Incoming!" Tim yells. I grab my keys and mutter something about insurance. I hate the thought of being there when all of our stuff is brought in. We have some nice things, but it all looks extremely tacky when it's sitting on the front lawn. The whole scene reeks of repossession.

I am about halfway around the circle when my cell phone rings.

It's Tim. He isn't speaking. He's making a "gh" sound like he's trying to pick up a Greek inflection and bring up a loogie.

"What!" I yell into the phone, even louder than I normally scream into my cell phone. "Tim!"

"The . . . pi . . . a . . . no!" he manages to gurgle out.

"What! What happened to the piano?"

"It's smashed to bits! It's destroy-o-o-o-o-oyed!"

It takes me two exits of New Circle and a side street to get the facts out of him. The movers have brought in our baby grand piano, and instead of it being in two pieces, carefully separated and wrapped in quilted blankies, it was in three gouged, nicked, bent, and broken pieces, plus ten thousand miniscule screws. Instead of removing the lid and packing it separately, our crack moving team in New Jersey had apparently decided it would be okay to just slide that big, black mother right onto the truck.

The evidence showed that sometime during the move the piano top flipped up and was wrenched off the top, splitting in two and sending a rainbow of tiny gold screws through the atmosphere. The circumstantial evidence is that there was one hell of a party on our moving van somewhere between New Jersey and Kentucky. I suspect Parkersburg, West Virginia. I half expected to find Polaroids of our moving crew posed in their underwear on our piano, using our lamps as microphones and Jack's tennis rackets as guitars.

I get to the insurance office, sign the papers, and drive home, all in a fog. I can't imagine what I'm going to find when I get back home. What I find are six very sheepish movers silently continuing to unload the truck and Tim sitting on the floor of the study, the phone in one hand and a box cutter in the other. His eyes frighten me. A voice is coming over the phone, saying, "Breathe . . . breathe . . . "

For the next several hours, five of our standing lamps come in, none of them in boxes and all of them bent to form letters of the alphabet. I think they are trying to spell S-A-T-A-N. Clearly he was at work here. A box comes in with a big hole in its side, looking like it had been set inches in front of a pitching machine and then stomped on by big boys in cleats. I go to the study to stop Tim from rigging a gallows from the ceiling fan, and behind me I hear a tinkling of glass as our coffee table top is unwrapped.

This is my worst moving nightmare.

By afternoon, we have watched helplessly as our cherry computer cabinet falls apart (not that it mattered; the door that fell off was gouged and scratched), our headboard comes in missing a top finial, and a printer explodes, sending ink everywhere. And then the moving company executives start calling, fruit baskets are ordered, and two guys in suits drive in from Louisville to personally lick the dirt from the bottom of my Nikes and take some photos. By this time, I have been upgraded to Mrs. Fitzpatrick and I am someone to be both pitied and knelt before in homage. My stuff has been badly abused. And some things are missing. Some key things, including all the hardware to put together Jack's bunk beds. The guys in suits scramble to replace it, but can't. They agree that, yes, without the hardware Jack's bed is just a pile of goddamn lumber. And seeing it lying there stacked in rows in his bedroom makes me think it is just that. (How much had we paid for that thing?)

In the end, we get several big checks, enough fruit to keep us regular for weeks, a nice dinner out, and an intimate relationship with a repairman, all compliments of the moving company, but not an explanation of what happened those fateful days in February in Parkersburg.

Tip #16: Don't be a fool. Your move will not go well unless you are supervising the movers as if they are toddlers in a non-Montessori preschool.

That move to Kentucky was our only really bad experience. Most of our other moves had only their fair share of breakage and missing things. Once, we had a picture frame come apart. Another time our bird bath cracked. In our move to Florida, the feet for the bottom of our TV went AWOL for two weeks but were eventually found in with some Playstation cords in a bedroom. In Illinois, we thought a mover took Tim's miniature plastic dresser with drawers full of screws and nuts and bolts, but we ended up finding it about two years later, in a box in the attic. These moves were more than smooth. They were downright velvety. Which is why I embarked on the Kentucky move with a casual air of someone who knew what she was doing.

"Are you going to move all the valuable stuff yourself?" a friend asked me.

"Hell no," I snorted. "These guys know what they're doing. They're movers. This is their business." While the guys packed our things and loaded the truck, I sat in the corner knitting a scarf and playing Game Boy Tetris. I trusted them. I thought if I bought them Subway sandwiches and Gatorade, they would reciprocate by being nice to my things. Plus, I'm the trusting type. My friend Gail, who is the opposite, once told our neighbor who was getting ready to move that he should hand carry his boxes of valuable hockey memorabilia. When he balked, she told him, "Okay, but put a bunch of Kotex on top of everything in the box. They'll never go through that."

After the move to Kentucky, I had to admit that Gail was at least a little bit right. I had been too trusting, lulled into a false sense of security by previous moves that had gone well. How had things gotten this complicated? I remember when Moving Day was singular—one day. When moving from one apartment to the next, we'd wake up about noon, call our pickup-truck-owner friend Mark, throw our things into a couple of boxes, have a couple of beers, go get pizza, drive to the new place, have a couple of beers, unload the truck, have a couple of beers, and send the extra pizza home with Mark as a token of our appreciation.

Then our family grew, the size of our houses grew, and we started to accumulate so much stuff. Fifteen years later, we now fill two large moving vans, and it takes about three weeks to pack, load, transport, unload, and unpack our things. People have earned college credits in the time it takes us to relocate. Which brings me to . . .

Tip #17: During the actual move, pretend like you're holing up for the apocalypse. You're not too far off.

If you're moving from a house bigger than a minivan, your move is going to take a long time. If you're handling your own packing, you'll need to start packing the lesser-used things months in advance. You'll soon find out how badly you don't need the bread machine, your curling iron, all things made of glass, and essentially 90 percent of the gifts you've received since you got engaged.

When the moving crews arrive, the process sometimes takes so long, your children will still be going to school, and you'll have to do things like wash an occasional face. Thus the need for packing things you'll need to use, things that can't be packed into boxes by the movers. We pack suitcases and set them in a corner or a room with signs that say "DO NOT PACK THIS STUFF," but I always forget something important. Once I forgot to set aside towels, and we had to dry ourselves with toilet paper. I always forget to set aside cleaning supplies to clean the house after it's emptied, so I end up spending a week's salary on a bucket, a broom, rags, Lysol, paper towels, Windex, and—if our neighbors refuse to answer their doors, knowing I'm about to borrow something else—occasionally even a new vacuum cleaner.

The kids usually have homework to do. Even though it's an unspoken rule that until your senior year of high school your grades don't really transfer well from school to school, my children remained studious to the bitter end. Once I had to buy Caroline a set of modeling clay, a poster board, toothpicks, a bag of plastic knives, and a dictionary to do an ancient Egypt project that she worked on while movers were swarming around her. And it about killed me because I knew we had all those things in boxes on the truck, including the plastic knives.

We try to evacuate the house while the movers are there, but it's not easy finding other places to go. You feel like a homeless person, and in truth you are. What is your true address during a move? You don't really have one. We discovered this the hard way during our move from Virginia to Ohio when Michael and Jack were young. On the day our movers arrived, the kids and I set up house-keeping in the public library. We played hide-and-seek in the magazines and took turns nap-ping on the couch in the fiction lounge. Jack was beginning to become emotionally attached to the stuffed Babar and Pokey Little Puppy that we bor-rowed from the children's story-time area. That night we all slept in a hotel, and the kids got their second wind and talked Tim into playing a game of Bed Jumping. They were having a grand time until Tim hit the bed in a bad way and threw out his back.

The drive to Ohio the next morning was pain-ful for him, and we stopped at my mother's house to spend that night. Tim walked into my mom's house, took a heating pad and ice pack, and stretched out on the floor in a narrow hallway of my mom's house, the only place where an electrical outlet was available. Michael and Jack were still in high gear from the hotel bed jumping game and started a new game of Monster, with Tim taking the title role, Jack being the victim and Michael being the rescuer. I played the part of the mom who was tired and pregnant and hadn't slept well in the hotel the night before and had greasy hair and ugly clothes on. My mom and I were in the kitchen talking when we heard Jack let out a scream. Apparently the monster had him by one arm and the rescuer had him by the other, and the victim now had what sounded like a broken arm. I came in, Tim struggled up, and we poked and prodded and asked Jack questions and decided his arm was broken.

Sometime during the fifteen-minute drive to the hospital emergency room, Tim and I looked at each other and realized how ridiculously homeless we looked—and were. We pleaded with Jack not to make up a story of child abuse, which was his thing to do that year. Dang it, why didn't we work on this before now? Toddlers don't know how to lie? My ass. Every bump and bruise he got was reportedly from me, Tim, or his older brother hitting him, punching him, or tripping him "again." We could imagine him telling the ER triage nurse, "My dad broke my arm—*again*." One look at us with our bad outfits and dirty hair, and Jack would be safely in foster care but fast.

We were a motley crew entering the ER, Tim walking like he had a board strapped to his back, me waddling in like I had shoplifted a basketball, and Jack looking like he had just had his arm broken by a family member (pick one).

"Address?" the woman behind the desk asked us at registration.

Tim and I looked at one another blankly. We officially were out of our old house and hadn't been given an apartment address yet.

"Just put my mom's house," I wearily told Tim, who was craning his neck to see where they were taking Jack for questioning.

As it turns out, we weren't in trouble. Jack only had nursemaid's elbow, which was easily popped back into place. It was done so quickly, he never had a chance to tell his tale of the beatings. And apparently, it's not unusual for homeless people to hang out at the North Side Hospital emergency room. We met some people whose straits were direr than ours, which bucked us up a bit.

"See, I told you we'd meet some nice people in this move," Tim said, cheerfully, as we drove away.

At that point, new acquaintances from a move meant the moving crew guys, some who were picked up off the street, many whose teeth numbered in the single digits, and some whose only skills were to smoke cigarettes and break things. These guys usually start off very friendly. Like you, they have high hopes of a good experience. You have to like and trust them. These are the men who are going to ensure that my mammogram films make it to the new house without too many fingerprints on them. These are men who are going to pack my most intimate possessions. Anything you have hidden in your bedroom nightstand drawer will be not only seen and touched by them, but listed on an inventory sheet in big black marker.

The honeymoon starts to end once they see the junk that you'll be taking. I try to stay clear of the guy who is assigned to pack the basement because he's down there alone in bad light, stewing over the fact that we're taking to the new place a bunch of duplicate toys, seventeen baskets with large space-hogging handles, a bag of conch shells from a trip to South Carolina three years ago that still smells of rotting sea life, and two broken computers.

When he does emerge from the basement to track you down, he'll ask, "Is everything down there going?" He's got a clip to his voice, as if he's talking through slightly clenched teeth and all his jaw muscles are as tight as they can be.

"Yes, like I said before, everything that's still down there needs to be packed. It's going."

"There is a pile of tree branches down there." He's not making eye contact with me and is looking at a spot high on the wall.

"You mean our stick collection? Yes, it goes."

And on it went.

"Yes, all four parts of the broken sewing machine cabinet go."

"Yes, the badly warped Barry Manilow albums go."

"Yes, the sixty-pound box of company stationery with the name *Timothy Fitzputrick* printed on it goes."

I was determined that my children should not suffer any more than they already had to. Why should they do without packrat junk just because we make them move a lot? Other kids have basements full of stuff no one uses, why shouldn't our kids? I was alone on this front. My husband agreed with the mover we had nicknamed Willie Nelson and thought that we should use our move to try to get rid of some of our junk. Willie and Tim both suggested a nice neighborhood yard sale. But I hung on with determination. I had assured the kids that we were taking every single possession of ours, for better or worse.

We had a Little Tykes playhouse that we got when all the kids were small enough to fit into it, and it had made several moves with us already. Then the kids got older and bigger and took to using the roof to launch crash cars. Then they got even older, and the playhouse gathered dust in our basement. Tim had been after me to get rid of it for years, even offering it to small kids in our neighborhood and trying to sneak it up the basement steps to other people's backyards. But I hung onto that playhouse with a vengeance. Getting rid of the playhouse would have been tantamount to admitting that our kids were not babies anymore, that I was a Mother of Older Kids now. When we moved from south Jersey to north Jersey I went through my normal routine—"Yes, the Little Tykes playhouse goes." When the head mover came into my corner to tell me the truck was all packed and ready to go, I looked out the front window and saw a problem. The huge moving van was out front, engine idling, and strapped to the back with bungee cords was the Little Tykes playhouse.

"We just barely had enough room to fit you into one truck," he said. "In fact, we had to strap that little playhouse onto the back."

"Oh, no, you can't do that," I said, putting down my knitting and taking out my earphones. "You can't pull up to the new house with that thing hanging off the truck. That's all my husband needs. He's been saying we have too much useless stuff, and now if he sees this, he'll know he's right."

I found out that day that even though I'm the boss, the client, the caller of shots on Moving Day, once the big truck has ignition, the crew will not unpack the truck and exchange a Little Tykes playhouse with something else to strap on the back. Fitting all your stuff into a semi is an engineering feat, like creating a 3-D jigsaw puzzle and then solving it. Movers are proud of their work, and they don't want to hear complaints from you when a longstanding marital issue rears its ugly head over whatever is strapped onto the back of the truck.

Tip #18: Six months before your move, stop buying all liquids and flammables, and get busy drinking that liquor.

When the moving van pulls away from your house, you would think there'd be some relief, maybe some sense that this moving machine is working. You would think. But, instead, you've moved on to the next problem, trying to figure out how you're going to fit into your car all the things the movers refused to take. And depending on how many stick and shell collections they had to pack, they're going to come up with all kinds of reasons why they can't take a third of your possessions. No matches, no lighters, no propane tanks, no aerosol cans, nothing flammable. No liquids, hazardous or otherwise; nothing that has been opened and isn't factory sealed.

"You're kidding, right?" I said, looking at the pile the packers had made of things they weren't packing. It was enormous. Vinegar, cooking oil, Lysol, Windex, spray starch, nail polish remover, mouthwash, hairspray, Pepto Bismal, antifreeze. This included everything I had just purchased at Costco, buying the mega containers to save seven cents. Some of those containers looked like props from *Honey I Shrunk the Kids*. Ironically, the pile also included a fire extinguisher, which falls into the broad category of an aerosol. The movers looked at this pile and saw flames and destruction. I saw dollar signs. I was already imagining the shopping trip I was going to have to make to replace all this.

"If something happens and it spills, it could ruin your whole load," the mover we'd named Flav-A-Flav tells me.

"Really?" I'm incredulous. "This 0.03-ounce bottle of Visine could ruin all my things?"

"It's the rule," says Flav, "and it was all spelled out in the brochure we sent you a month ago."

Ah yes, the brochure. On the cover was a picture of a sparkling moving van parked in front of a beautiful, white Cape Cod house on a bright, sunny day. The first page was a letter from the president of the moving company assuring me that all my needs would be taken care of by a professional staff of relocation specialists. He gently ordered me to relax. Then it told the story of the Smiths, a cute-as-a button family who is moving from St. Louis to Denver. Mrs. Smith is wearing hip-hugger jeans, a black tank top, a good bra, and a belt that matches and fits her. She has had a haircut in the past week. Mr. Smith has his shirt tucked in and is wearing stylish glasses. They're both beaming from ear to ear, apparently overwhelmed with the efficiency of their moving company. Either that or they're on an acid trip and are hallucinating that they're already in Denver.

"For the Smiths' move," the brochure says, "the van that carries their household goods might well be on a longer trip—from Memphis to Boise, for example. It's not unusual for the shipments of more than one family to be transported on a single moving van. Don't worry that your goods will be mixed up with another family's shipment, however. Van lines employ sophisticated techniques to identify different customers' possessions and to keep them separate inside the van."

Right. Those "sophisticated techniques" would be the little colored stickers.

I'd love to meet the author of this brochure. I can picture him doubled over with laughter as he typed the word "sophisticated." He uses it two more times in the booklet, once to describe the packing process and again in discussing the inventory sheets. He's a hoot, that guy.

We follow the Smiths throughout their move, from Preparing Your Children for the Move (the Smiths gave their children age-appropriate tasks to perform to make them feel a part of the process) to Computers and Other Electronics (Mr. Smith disconnected wires attached to movable hardware such as a modem or mouse and parked his PC by inserting a blank floppy disk into the disk drive).

In my standoff with Flav-A-Flav, I mentally flip through the brochure, vaguely remembering a cartoon illustration of a big pile of things, much like the pile of liquids and flammables sitting before me except that some of the containers had skulls and crossbones on them in the brochure, with a big red circle with a line through it. The picture of the Smiths' pile of liquids and flammables, however, were clean and had lids. None of their cooking oil jugs were closed on top with a baggie and athletic tape, and none of their peroxide bottles were stoppered with a Ken doll head. And the Smiths didn't have any half-full bottles of scotch to deal with, either.

"The Jack Daniels can't go?" I ask. Liquor is both a liquid and a flammable, it seems. The big kahuna of moving bad boys. Flav-A-Flav just looks at me with sad, sober eyes, and then I get it. They're hoping we're going to give them this stuff to take home. Well, forget it. I've done that. Our Illinois movers had me toting boxes of liquids and flammables to their cars as they haggled over dividing it. They took sealed bids for my brother Jeff's homemade honey. These guys' wives haven't purchased a single liquid or flammable since they started working for the moving company.

Flav and his crew hadn't impressed me all that much, so I told them to leave the pile, and I'd deal with it. I considered actually consuming it all right then and there, just for spite, but was afraid of bursting into toxic flames. Some of it I gave to our real estate agent, who was coming by to check on me. (Or was she? Perhaps she had her eye on the fireplace matches and the sixty-four ounce bottle of Listerine.) The rest I tried to cram into our car, already full of our suitcases for temporarily living, the cleaning supplies we needed, some perishable foods I could not part with, the kids' backpacks, and three plants we were trying to save.

"Just leave that stuff here," Tim told me when he saw the box of things unfit for the moving van. "We'll just buy new when we get there."

The miser in me couldn't come to grips with that. I started opening zippered compartments of my big suitcase and shoving in bottles of whatever I could fit. I was kneeling on the back of the SUV, pushing with all my might a bottle of vanilla extract into a nook when I started laughing. Or crying. I couldn't tell. It struck me as extremely funny and/or sad that I was so bent on saving this bottle of vanilla, as well as the other things in the pile. It was of utmost importance that they all come along with us. *Don't worry. I won't leave you behind*! I was sending a mental message to the pile. *Not without my liquids and flammables!*

Moving hysteria can be funny like that. Weird funny, not ha ha funny. Now that I think of it, maybe that's what was happening to the Smiths when they got their picture snapped for the brochure.

Tip #19: Once Move-Out Day is over, get geared up for Move-In Day. It's the same except you have to wear lipstick.

As bad as Move-Out Day is, Move-In Day has added repercussions. On your way out, you need not worry about making impressions. You can always choose to never see those people again. Your entrance to your next place, however, is another story. Remember what your mother told you about first impressions? Me neither. But I'll tell you this now: What your neighbors see when you pull your car into your new driveway and get out is how they'll talk about you forever, no matter how long you live there.

The Clampetts made a better first impression than we made moving to south Jersey. The day we pulled into our new neighborhood, Tim and I couldn't have been crankier. I had spent the previous night driving back and forth to Kmart to pay good money for things we already owned but couldn't put our hands on. I made a half-hearted attempt to sleep, on the floor in a toddler-sized *101 Dalmatians* sleeping bag that I had to share with the dog. Tim had eaten half a box of macaroni and cheese for dinner, prepared with water and Crisco substituted for the milk and butter we didn't have and that I kept forgetting to pick up at Kmart.

I had hoped to sneak in and at least empty the minivan of the McDonald's food bags or maybe look in a mirror that wasn't the rearview kind. Instead, as we pulled into our new driveway, it was flanked by our new neighbors, Ginger and Mary Ann. I was, at best, a younger and skankier Mrs. Howell, in a wrinkly turquoise jogging suit, nonsymmetrical pigtails, and my glasses from 1983.

Remember the movie *Terms of Endearment*? When Deborah Winger and her husband start their drive to their new home, she looks like the movie star she is. Cut to the scene where the car is pulling up to the new place. Her hair is stringy, and she's wearing glasses. The person who wrote that script knew that detail would resonate with anyone who has moved. It's a known fact that contact lenses hurt on Moving Day. Sometimes you can't find your regular glasses, and you have to dig around to find those old, tortoiseshell Larry King specs from college. That's how your new neighbors will always remember you.

I sat in the van for a few minutes, afraid to get out and face the female cast of Gilligan's Island. As I opened my door, Jack opened his and out fell a big pile of used Kleenexes, a pudding pop wrapper, and three shoes.

Ginger and Mary Ann were smiling and staring at us, soaking us in. Their husbands and a few more neighbors were beginning to stroll over. In the next two hours, I'd be asking these people to babysit my kids while I orchestrated the unloading of our things, as well as give me their Social Security numbers and mothers' maiden names for the emergency contact card at school. How I handled these next few minutes would determine whether they would say yes or scurry home and lock their doors.

A couple of years later, when it was safe to talk about that day, those same neighbors told me their first impression of me wasn't bad. (They didn't elaborate. And I think I heard a snicker when someone muttered, " . . . glasses . . . .") But they said their first impression of Tim was bad.

"He drove in all cranky," Ginger's husband said. This from a man who was still whining about moving once, seven years earlier, a move from ten miles away that didn't involve a single sleeping bag or fast-food order. Tim and I didn't care. We had our contacts in, and our self-esteem was back.

Tip #20: Don't be a martyr. Let the pros unpack for you. It's what they went to the vo-tech for.

If your corporate relocation includes an offer to unpack your things, take it. Your relo specialist and moving crew leader will try to tell you the unpacking is a bad, bad thing. They are lying. It's only a bad thing for them. It's a good thing for you.

"They don't put anything away, you know," they'll tell you. "They'll just set it down on the counter or on the floor." They say this like having all your stuff in piles on the floor is far worse than having all your stuff inside packing materials and boxes on the floor.

Trust me, you want the unpacking, especially if it's part of your package, and you don't have to pay for it. Having the moving crew unpack for you is the only way you'll be able to notice that some things are broken in time to put in a claim, and it's the only way you'll be able to find half of the essentials that you've gone far too long without.

A major benefit in the unpacking deal is that they take away the empty boxes and packing materials. You'll have a hard enough time wading through all of your belongings. Add to that a bunch of boxes and enough brown paper to fill Soldier Field, and you run the risk of actually losing a small child or pet.

Even with the unpacking option, you will eventually have to put things where they belong. This can be a stomach-turning task. Your house will look a lot like Barbie and Ken's place after it's been folded up and put back in the basement: hair accessories, wine glasses, the car registration, and a golf club piled up in the kitchen.

You'll be overwhelmed with piles of stuff that have to be put away. Everything will be in the wrong room and in the wrong place, unless of course its rightful place is in the middle of the foyer floor. You'll be inclined to use normal everyday organizational skills and put things into piles. *Avoid this temptation.* If you use the pile system, you'll have sub-piles and auxiliary piles. You'll run out of room, and the piles will start commingling and interbreeding. You'll start to have piles of offspring, and soon your strategy will require you stopping to hook up the computer to set up an Excel spreadsheet just to organize the piles. Hours later, you'll find yourself in a room surrounded by the same junk, only in different spots. You will have nothing to cross off your list.

Instead, take one thing at a time. Pick up one item only, say a paperclip. Walk it over to where it belongs. Put it there, inhale, and wallow for a moment in the satisfaction that you've just accomplished something. Then go back to ground zero and pick up another single thing. Maybe a spoon. Repeat until you get hungry and have cleared an exit path to the pizza delivery phone number.

CHAPTER 6

Just Like the Witness Protection Program But with Fewer Toys

Temporary Living During a Move

"Okay, guys, pick out three toys to take to the apartment," I tell Michael and Jack. It's Christmas night. They look at me with disbelief. Three toys? How can they possibly choose between the Aladdin snake stick with the red, glowing eyes and Hungry Hungry Hippos? And does the 160-piece Fisher Price zoo count as one toy or 160 toys? Michael is distressed. I'm not

worried about Jack, knowing that as long as he has his blankie and at least one thumb, we could send him to Attica for the next month, and he'd be okay.

We are packing up and heading out, moving from Virginia to Ohio. Except it's never quite that simple. We bought a new house, and before we can move in, the builder has to add steps up to the doors, install light fixtures, and put some appliances in the kitchen. This necessitates a temporary apartment for us for a couple of weeks. The choosing of the toys, which violates every maternal instinct I have, is the last gut-wrenching straw for me. I have had to divide all our possessions into 1) things we need for the trip, which we'll have to fit into our non-minivan car, 2) things we need for the next four weeks in our temporary apartment, and 3) things we can do without until we get into the house—which will be put into storage.

Tim has attempted to form a fourth pile— things we can do without forever—and has tried to sneak these to the curb on garbage day, but the wailing reached new, ear-splitting levels, so he abandoned that pursuit. I have a colossal headache, and now the boys are crying. Not because they have to choose three toys, but because Tim is starting to take down the Christmas tree. I'm near tears myself. Tim is whistling "Up on the Housetop." Being the guy who can't wait to get on to the next thing, he is openly joyous. He finally has a good excuse to take the tree down while the chimney is still warm from Santa's ascent. We suspect this has long been his dream.

"Everything is going to be okay, you guys," I tell the boys, holding them close to me. They think I'm hugging them, but I'm actually shielding their view of Tim swatting at the treetop angel with the Aladdin snake stick.

"Hey, remember, what I told you?" I tell the boys excitedly. "The apartment has cable!"

They instantly cheer up. It is 1992, and I am still the type of parent who has more on my list of "Don'ts" than on my list of "Oh-What-the-Hell-It's-Not-Going-to-Kill-Thems." We don't have cable television, meaning our children are reduced to watching fuzzy, grainy PBS, soap operas, and that show where the white guy with an Afro teaches you how to paint. I have told the boys about this place called The Apartment, a wonderful, magical place where there would be more channels than you can imagine, and all of them clear enough to see. I tell them that during those four weeks of temporary living, they can watch as much TV as they want. Who needs a Fisher Price zoo?

Tip #21: Think hard: What will you need until you can get at your storage stash? You're not thinking hard enough.

What I didn't mention to my boys was that although we'd have the best TV the '90s could offer, we would not have any two matching shoes, a telephone book, or a writing utensil of any kind. Dividing up our stuff had turned out to be harder than I had thought. It was as if a bunch of strangers from the School for the Blind had packed for us.

In all honesty, I don't know how I could have been expected to remember everything we would need for four weeks of living. You're talking about a family who once went to a golf outing weekend and forgot our golf clubs. We went to visit friends out of town and forgot any and all of Jack's shoes. We tend to plan our vacations by stopping at a

Walmart right off the bat, to pick up the things we forgot, like bathing suits in Florida and dress clothes at Easter.

You can't believe how much we as humans have evolved into mega-consumers until you try to live on a couple small boxes of stuff. You'll tell yourself you have a very simple life, full of simple pleasures and down-to-earth values. Then you'll realize that you use four products on the roots of your hair alone. And your husband is worse. Even though all of his suits are slightly varying shades of gray, he'll need four pair of shoes just for work.

When you start to pack for temporary living, you'll get partway through the job, and a silent alarm will go off in your brain saying, "That's enough!" Later you'll realize you hadn't even gotten to anything in the bedrooms.

When we got to our apartment in Ohio, it was a surprise to none of us that we were missing lots of things we needed. We had no emergency drugs for the sinus headache I would get from the dry heat in that place—a heat so dry that the pots of boiling water on the stove from 7:00 a.m. to midnight didn't help at all. I took to calling my new doctor and moaning out my self-diagnosis of either an aneurism or a brain tumor. We had no shorts for Michael that he could use for gym class. We had no spare car key, no calculator, no paperclips or stapler, and no boots, hats, or gloves, and it was late December in northeastern Ohio. We did have lots of other good stuff, though.

"Do we really need four rings of measuring spoons, all with only the one and a half tablespoon and one-sixteenth teaspoon on them?" Tim said, reaching into one of the boxes that had made it to the apartment. "And if not, why do we have them and not my toothbrush?"

Tip #22: Don't get too attached to your temporary life during a move. It's not sustainable.

Temporary apartment living is a necessary evil in the moving process. More often than not, it's impossible to coordinate moving out of one house with moving into another, mostly because lawyers are involved, and they love to see common folk suffer.

The apartments you're assigned by the relo company are usually the cheapest in town. We're not talking about luxury condo living here. The apartment is designed to house one lonely bachelor with no friends. Only one person can fit in the kitchen at a time, and I called it first—it wasn't going to be me. These places are certainly not built for children. In one of our apartments, the only eating surface—a small round table in a tiny eating area—had a glass top. A *glass top*. We were expected to let loose two single-digit-aged boys in that place.

Our apartments were supposed to be furnished, although only a family of circus freaks could live with what was in there. Three towels? One frying pan the size of a pancake? One pillow per person? *What kind of people do they think we are?*

Because there was no nine by thirteen-inch glass baking dish, and that's the only way I knew how to cook, we took to eating out a lot. I learned that KFC's popcorn chicken, which looked so yummy on the commercials, is actually the little bits of skin and batter that fall to the bottom of the fryer. I think it's someone's actual job to scoop it out with a scraper and place it in little cardboard treasure chests. I had yearned for an excuse to spend $5.99 on it ever since I first saw the commercial, and here I was eating it. And here I was feeling ill and vowing to join PETA as soon as I had a permanent address to put on my membership card.

The only meals I ever cooked in the apartments were Hamburger Helper and its other meat cousins, instant mashed potatoes, and a longtime favorite of my college roommates: macaroni and cheese with canned tuna. My husband and kids were not impressed with the menu choices. Michael still talks about it.

"Remember when Mom made Pork Helper?" is all he has to say to get Caroline to spit out whatever she has in her mouth.

Tim and the kids ate at the coffee table, while watching TV. I was limiting my bodily contact with the furniture, so I ate standing up in front of the ironing board. Yes, oddly the apartment had an ironing board.

The worst thing about temporary living is that it's so, well, *temporary.* You're eager to get on with your new life, the life where you take a shower before noon and never go to the grocery store without a top that matches your pants. The life where you dust and vacuum once a week with classical music playing and throw dinner parties with cloth napkins. Where you shop in the morning and have lunch with friends in the afternoon. But you can't start that life because you're living in an apartment with neighbors who are three drug dealers on one side and a just-divorced cretin with furniture from Rent-A-Center on the other side. And your own apartment has a film on the carpet and reeks of menthol cigarettes. You know that smell is hiding another one, far worse, but you don't want to pursue it.

I had no yard work to do, very little cooking to do (a Pork Helper dinner takes about fourteen minutes to prepare), and it seemed silly to do any real housework, since it didn't count for anything. I could feel myself getting sucked into my environment. I started to wear my ratty robe around the apartment and kept an unlit cigarette in the corner of my mouth.

I was spending hours making lists itemizing how grand my new life was going to be when I got in the house. This is going to be the house where I plant bulbs in the fall wearing flowery garden gloves and kneeling on one of those big sponges with a handle. This is the house where I'm going to put up framed black-and-white photographs. This is the house where I'm going to mount a calendar on the refrigerator, color-coded for each child's activities with stickers with symbols reminding me to give the dog her heartworm medicine (a little dog's face) and change the batteries in my smoke detector (flames).

The further down I sank in my temporary life, the grander my plans became for my new life. I knew I had hit rock bottom the day the two lives came full circle, and I started ordering knick-knacks from the Home Shopping Network.

The kids loved apartment living. Not just when they were little and had cable, but when they were older, too. It fulfilled some fantasy they had of being inner-city foster children. Even though I was always home, they asked for a key because they liked to play latchkey kids whose parents were out in a van making meth. They began carrying cans of spray paint in their backpacks and wearing do-rags.

Luckily we all snapped out of it when we left the apartment and got into our house. I never followed through with the color-coded calendar or the gardening, but I did quit pretending to smoke and sold the knick-knacks on eBay.

Remember, your life in that apartment counts for squat. Don't waste your time trying to adjust or even learning the address and phone number there. You'll never see those people again, unless you're buying drugs or looking for eligible bachelors.

C H A P T E R   7

Didn't We Used to Have Three Cats?
Moving Pets

It's Day Four of our move from Illinois to New Jersey, and I'm beginning to be a little concerned about Lipstick, Jack's goldfish. Four days earlier, the guys had come to pack, and we handed over the fish bowl, but wisely not before transferring Lipstick into a coffee can. I poked holes in the lid and remembered to set aside the fish food and put the whole aquatic assemblage into the Do Not Pack pile.

The fish was fine at first. He earned the unlikely name Lipstick because he was a tough little badass. About a year after we got "Goldy" as he was known then, I refilled his bowl using regular well water from our tap instead of distilled water. A couple of days later we noticed that Goldy wasn't gold anymore. He was see-through. You could see all his little internal organs and some stringy things. He looked like a diagram in a fish anatomy book. All of him had lost the goldish-orangish color except the very tip of his tail and his lips. I had not been aware that fish had lips, except for Mr. Limpet, of course. Jack's fish looked like he was wearing my mom's Orange Rage resurrected from the 1965 Avon catalog. I guess the mineral-rich well water had bleached out most of the pigment in his body except for his two extremities. He looked so cute that we renamed him Lipstick (clearly, Goldy wasn't going to work anymore and Transparent just didn't sound right).

Because of his rep, I figure Lipstick will be fine in a coffee can for our move. The days of packing are followed by days of loading the truck, and then we get in the car to make the drive to New Jersey.

"The water is sloshing out!" I can hear Jack say from the backseat after three hours' driving.

"Is the lid on?" Jeez, I had only poked a couple of holes. And we hadn't taken time to add to the water, so it had to be pretty shallow by now.

"I can't find the lid," Jack says, his voice muffled as he digs around the muck of the backseat, which includes our dog Spanky, a tank with Michael's two aquatic frogs, and who knows what other living things that may have jumped into the car while we were at the rest stop.

"Try not to hit any more bumps, Mom," Michael suggests. Good idea. We only have five hundred more miles to go. With highway conditions in Ohio and Pennsylvania what they are, we should be fine.

By the time we arrive in New Jersey, most of the water is still in the can, and we eventually unearth the lid from layers of debris in the backseat. But it takes four more days for our stuff to arrive at the house and get unloaded and unpacked. Lipstick's care and attention is low on the priority list. By the time we locate the box with the fishbowl, Lipstick is swimming in murky, rusty water with a film of greenish-brown slime on top. He survives, though, and seems happy to finally be back in his bowl with the colorful stones in the bottom and the ceramic treasure chest and miniature shipwreck. (Note: Lipstick lived another two years, surviving a big gash on his side and several bowl-cleaning accidents that involved him flopping around on the bathroom counter dangerously close to the sink drain. This fish had been through so much abuse, we think he was acting out by smoking crack and cutting himself. Sadly, however, he never had a chance to move again with us. He turned up dead on the day we had Spanky put to sleep. We think it was a euthanasia-suicide pact.)

Tip #23: Don't underestimate the power of your pet's maladjustment.

I've heard about these people who give their dogs away because they're moving, and they can't take them. I can't imagine doing that to my children, but will I get credit for that? Surely not. I feel bad enough about the pet corpses we had to leave. In the woods behind our house in Illinois are the tiny graves of frogs Kaney and Speckle, goldfish Goldy Sr., and tadpole Eckie, all marked by Popsicle-stick crosses. I had to talk myself out of exhuming the bodies and taking them to new graves at our new house.

Only once did I give away a pet before a move, and that was our parrot Black Sam Bellamy. His refusal to talk and play well with others—namely Michael, our only child at the time—made it very easy to sell him before we moved. Maybe birds don't carry the same family status, or maybe I was just maxed out on guilt about moving Michael away from his favorite cousins, but I didn't feel one ounce of regret about leaving that silent bird.

For all of our other pets, I gladly crammed dogs and sea creatures into cars, vans, and SUVs to get them from one house to another. We've made extra stops so they can do things like drink water and go to the bathroom. They're rarely appreciative and not supportive at all. Our dog Spanky, when arriving at our house in New Jersey, decided she didn't like linoleum floors and refused to walk in our kitchen—a problem, since the back door and her rightful running space went out from there. We had to walk her around from the side door.

We brought her dish to the edge of the family room and she would crane her neck over the dividing line, carefully keeping her front paws on the carpeted area. It took her about a week before she felt her point had been made: *How could you move from a house with hardwood in the kitchen to one with tacky linoleum? Are we moving up, or what's the deal here?*

Our next dog Grace made three moves with us. She was stoic, but we think she was saving up complaints to present to us when she learned how to use the computer. She had to stay in kennels while the movers were at our house since they have an open door policy—literally taking the doors off the hinges. Grace would have walked right out the door and never come back, but not before biting every moving guy in the crotch.

For one of Gracie's moves, we had to pick her up from one kennel and drive her to the new town, to a new kennel, with only a cramped car ride in between for her to voice her complaints and decompress from the horrors of imprisonment. Moving to north Jersey, the kennel was our first stop when we drove into town. *No, I won't go back*, her eyes pleaded with me as I tried to get her out of the car. I told the kennel guy she was bad with other dogs.

"She fights, but only with other animals. With people, she's fine if you don't mind being licked," I said. "And she's cranky because we're moving."

They put a little red bandana around her neck, which struck me cute until I realized that was a kennel symbol for Doesn't Play Well with Others. Or Goes for the Throat in Dog Fights. When I left her, she was standing at the fence in solitary, all gang-like in her bandana, staring me down.

When we were able to keep her in our temporary apartment in Kentucky, Grace was like a caged lion, unaccustomed to being in small spaces and not at all liking the fact that we were on the second floor and she couldn't just stroll out the door and wander around a fenced-in backyard. She hated looking out of our big, glass living room window at that fat, black lab below, running loose just out of her reach. I had to put Grace on a humiliating leash and walk her four times a day. She was afraid of the open-backed stairs that led down to the ground level. She hated pooping in the cold snow while traffic whizzed by. In so many facial expressions, she made her point clear: *Moving sucks for the dog.*

From what I understand, cats are different. They don't seem to stress out about anything. Cat owners seem to be less concerned about their pets' adjustment, and sometimes don't even take them along. I know two people who moved out of state and left a note on the kitchen counter saying their cat wasn't moving with them and was meandering around the neighborhood somewhere.

"If you see a gray and white tabby, please tell him we've moved, and he should've come home when we called him." What part of *Here, kitty, kitty, kitty* did he not understand?

Dogs, however, are stressful creatures of habit. Moving to another house upsets their daily routine, the eat-sleep-gotothebathroom-getatreat machine that runs nonstop. I can't understand why there are not more drugs available for pets that are going through a stressful time like moving. When people get stressed out, doctors are all over each other writing prescriptions for "something to take the edge off." When your dog is anxious because of a sudden kitchen floor change, the vet will reluctantly offer some wimpy herbal thing and then warn you not to overuse it. Why not? Is there a chance that my dog will become an herb addict? Will she resort to increasingly violent crime just to get her paws on more? Maybe resort to prostitution or behavior even sluttier than she already exhibits? Would I even recognize if she was going through severe herb withdrawal, based on her normal behavior, which already includes whimpering and twitching in her sleep?

They say animals can sense change coming, and I think that's true. Plus, you don't have to be very high on the evolutionary chart to figure out that when all the furniture goes onto a truck, the Alpo isn't going to hit the dog dish in your old spot that night. Our dogs got a little bit antsy when they saw us put things in piles. They would do the thunderstorm pace, weaving methodically throughout the house, waiting for something to happen. After moving three times, whenever our dog saw that I was doing as much as a good spring cleaning, she would start looking for her bandana.

Tip #24: Don't rely on your dog for any sympathy whatsoever.

If you're a dog owner, chances are your expectations are set pretty low to begin with. Your house is covered with muddy paw prints, the legs of your good furniture have chew marks, and your clothes are covered with fur. Don't think that moving is going to suddenly turn your dog into a helpmate. Dogs are not going to offer you any aid or comfort. They'll already be ticked off about changes in their sleep schedule and location, changes in which they had no input whatsoever. They may use the move as an excuse to "forget" how to be house-trained, claiming that green carpet in the family room looks an awful lot like grass. If you're a cat owner, expect even less. You have my sympathy.

Tip #25: Here's the good news: A dog will help you make new friends fast. Enemies, too, but—did I mention friends?

If you can't get your hands on a baby or a two-seater sports car at the time of your move, a dog will suffice in impressing your new neighbors and friends. A dog will expand your pool of potential acquaintances with the addition of dog parks, veterinarians' office waiting rooms, boarding kennels, and the pet food aisle at the grocery store.

A dog will help to set your family's image in everyone's minds. If you can help it, have a nice dog, preferably a retriever or lab or some fluffy mutt, as opposed to a pit bull, which will help set your family's image as Conspiracy Theorists Who Will Soon Build an Underground Bunker In Spite of Homeowner Association Rules and Regs.

I moved three times with Grace, who despite her serene, classy name was a clumsy, raunchy Akita, one of the Five Dog Breeds You Really Shouldn't Have When You Move. Getting homeowners' insurance with an Akita is a dicey operation. Even if you are willing to sign a form swearing that you'll never make a claim related to said grumpy, attitudinal dog, the insurance agent who comes out to your new house to take a look-see will not want to see an Akita, a Doberman, a pit bull, a German Shepherd, or a Rottweiler.

Hiding a ninety-pound Akita from an insurance agent three times takes its toll. I wasn't able to hide her from our new neighbors, and I'm sure they formed a few choice opinions about us based on our choice of dogs. I had to make it up by organizing the block party two years in a row and fertilizing the bejeezus out of our front lawn.

CHAPTER 8

But I Thought You Packed the Cigarettes and Condoms

What We Leave Behind in a Move

Michael and I are sitting on the couch in the family room, looking at an old photo album.

"There's our old backyard! Remember the cool woods we had back there?" I say. "Remember the times we camped out in those woods?"

"Yeah," Michael says. "And remember the time we camped out there with my Cub Scout troop, and you told that scary story, and that one kid

was crying and you had to call his mom to come and pick him up?"

I turn the page. I had forgotten about my stint as den mother. A miserable example of my unwillingness to recognize that young children can't handle a simple urban legend. We flip backward until we come across pictures of our house in Ohio.

"Remember the cool bunk beds you and Jack had when you shared a room in that house?" I ask Michael.

"Yeah, and remember that little trap door in the ceiling of my hide-out cubby in my closet? I remember going in there and opening that trap door and looking up in the attic at all the boxes up there."

I freeze. The boxes? What boxes?

"What boxes?" I ask Michael, tentatively.

"There were all these boxes up there. In the attic. In our house in North Canton."

That can't be right. That was a brand new house, still had sawdust in the corners, when we moved into it. If there were boxes in that attic, they had to belong to us. And I don't remember them. I don't remember putting them up there.

More importantly, I don't remember taking them out of there.

Oh, my God, we left boxes of stuff in our house in Ohio! I run to the garage to find Tim.

"Tim! What have we been missing? For the past six years, what have we been missing?"

Tim looks up from the lawn mower and squints at me. What the hell am I talking about? "Your brain," he mutters, pretty pleased with himself for yet another fourth-grade humor comeback, and turns back to his work.

"No, really! Michael just told me that when he used to peek up into the attic from that trap door in his closet, he saw boxes. Do you remember storing things in that attic?"

Tim looks up again. "It's possible."

"But what was in the boxes? What did we leave there? It could have been something really, really important!"

And of course you know what Tim's response is. If it was so important, wouldn't we have needed it, or at least noticed it wasn't around anymore, sometime over the past six years?

For the days, weeks, months, and years since, I've tried to figure out what is in those boxes. I've been tempted to track down the people who live there now and ask them to take a quick look into that attic and let me know what's up there. I'm sure that by now someone has discovered them. You don't put a trap door within reach of a little raised cubby hideout in the closet of a kids' room and not open the door over a period of six years.

One part of me wants them back in the worst way. I have a fantasy involving a shoebox full of gold bouillon or bearer bonds, despite the fact that I have never owned or even seen either of those things. Actually, I'm not even sure what they are. Another part of me knows that by leaving those boxes, we left our mark on that house. And leaving your mark is part of the good, sentimental side of moving. Much like the way our dog marks her territory by peeing and the way my kids spit on their food so no one else will want a bite, we like to leave our own mark, scent, or bodily fluid on the places we've been.

Tip #26: Leaving unwanted junk is fair game. Don't leave any good stuff.

When you do the final walk-through of your empty house with your movers, don't let them fool you. They have to take everything, even if the truck is full and is starting to coast down the street. Stand your ground. They're very good at playing dumb. You can tell the head honcho every twenty-five minutes that the big umbrella table "goes," yet when he says he's done, and you see it still standing alone in the backyard, he'll turn on that surprised look.

"Oh, you're taking *that, too?*" he'll say. "But it looks so nice right here!"

Don't fall for it. And don't let him convince you that it would look even better in his own backyard.

You'll be leaving enough, trust me. Even if you clean up all the stains, marks, and gouges, your paint colors and wallpaper choices will speak volumes about you to the new owners, who are sure to hate them.

It's a bittersweet feeling when you find someone else's mark on a house that you move into. It's fun to imagine how the cherry red stain got on the white carpet of the family room (I'd like to think there were daiquiris and dancing involved, although cherry pop and jumping jacks sound fun, too) and why there are scallions growing in the front flower beds of my house in Kentucky (obsessed onion lovers or top soil that was brought in from a farm somewhere?). When you find pencil marks three feet up on a door frame with "Eric 1990" scrawled next to it, you can easily imagine Eric becoming as tall as a basketball guard by 2006 and stumbling into that same door frame as an eighteen-year-old, home from a night of drinking in the backseat of a car.

In our house in Youngstown, we reopened a closed-up old laundry chute and found two unopened condoms that had been carefully slid behind a board.

"Did this place used to be a frat house?" Tim asked.

In our houses, we've discovered packs of cigarettes hidden behind toilets and empty booze bottles stuffed behind boxes of floor tile in the basement. Discovering the evidence of past occupants helps you to see that real people—with real passions and vices, opinions, and bad taste—lived in the space you now occupy. It makes you see that your house has seen a lot. And it demands some respect for that. Right after a good cleaning with bleach.

Tip #27: Avoid anyone who has inherited your former home. You don't look all that good.

Because of the things you leave behind—and I'm not just talking about booze bottles and condoms, here—you're going to want to beat feet whenever you see the buyers of your former home. Don't go back to visit the old haunts. Avoid them at parties. Despite your best efforts to clean up that place, the people who moved in have quite literally invaded your space. It's like they're standing inches away from your face and have seen you naked in your bathroom talking to yourself and picking your nose.

Those squatters *know things about you.* They know the depth of your spring cleaning, or the lack thereof. They know what the neighbors remember about your behavior at the 2008 block party. They know what your dog did in the backyard. And they can deduce that you were a 1-800-LAWYERS call away from a divorce over your choice of master bathroom wallpaper.

If you live in one of our former houses, I'll never see you again, so let me clear up some of the mysteries right here. In Youngstown, the bedroom door that looks like someone fed the bottom end into a wood chipper was actually chewed by our dachshund, Schnitzel, who tried like the dickens to get into our bedroom during every thunderstorm for the two years we lived there. He was a couple of weather advisories away from chewing his way in when we moved.

In Cleveland, the dent in the dormer ceiling of one of the upstairs bedrooms (the dent that looks exactly like the top of Michael's head) was from a wild cousin sleepover with bed jumping and general cavorting. There may still be some hair and scalp fragments imbedded in there.

In Springfield, Virginia, those things that look like weeds that come up in the back bed are actually my first attempt to grow herbs. On second thought, they might be just weeds. And that pale gray stain on the white carpet upstairs is from a horrible stomach virus that swept through our house one bad winter. I've never looked at white carpet or mushroom pizza with the same innocence.

In North Canton, Ohio, there are, of course, the boxes in the attic, which I'm now thinking may contain some clips of mine from when I was a reporter. If you find them, could you please not laugh too hard at the picture of me that ran with my column? My nose was never that big. That was the photographer's mistake to use a fish-eye lens.

In Cary, Illinois, we left a variety of spills and marks, including a series of tempera paint stains on the family room carpet, where the kids were just indigo shy of a full rainbow. We almost left a tent in the garage attic. The movers missed it, despite my instructions on what was to "go." I realized as soon as we got unpacked that we didn't have the tent. Fortunately, the house hadn't been sold yet, and the locks hadn't been changed. I called our old neighbor Chris, who used the spare key they had for our house and spirited out the tent. He and his family have used it for sleepovers in the same backyard woods where we used to camp. He's been given strict instructions not to tell urban legends.

In Mount Laurel, New Jersey, there is a brown sandal, women's size seven, on the roof somewhere, belonging to one of Michael's friends from a swim party he had in the eighth grade.

In Sparta, New Jersey, those scratches on the fence are from our dog Grace, who used to climb and claw her way out of the yard to chase and bring home valuable groundhogs. And in the basement is the Little Tykes playhouse, Tim's victorious decision to finally leave that thing somewhere.

In Lexington, because we were downsizing to the basement-less matchbox in Florida that they claim is a cozy/charming seaside villa, we had to leave some really good stuff. But we hid it, so they would think we forgot it.

Who knows what we'll leave here in Florida. We've done our best, using whatever dog-vomit, Red Dye #2, and hard, missile-like objects we can find. If you get this house, don't expect any valuables, liquids, or flammables. I've finally figured out what I'm doing. And it all goes.

CHAPTER 9

You Know You're Not the New Kid Anymore When Your Mom Stops Buying You Cool Stuff

Getting the Children Adapted, Adjusted, and Settled in Their New Home

I'm walking . . . I'm walking . . . walking . . . through the halls of another elementary school, around corners, through doors, and I think in and out of two portable classrooms

(or "trailers" as they're called everywhere but in an academic setting). I finally arrive at the door I've been looking for—Guidance. That's definitely what I need. I'm at the school to register Jack and Caroline, who are at home taking advantage of being legally truant. We just moved in yesterday, and the kids are wallowing in the Fitzpatrick Law of the Moving Child: No one counts up how many days of school you've attended when you transfer to another district. We always take advantage of that rule, and I let the kids have a couple of days to find a spiral notebook and a sharpened pencil in the landfill that is their bedrooms before making them start school.

I use one day to get them registered and try to find my way around the school where I'll be soon shelving library books and handing out mystery meat tacos as a mom volunteer. I'm happy to see that hospital green and pumpkin orange are still the rage in school lockers. Those colors follow us wherever we go.

The guidance secretary looks up and smiles when I let myself into her office. I introduce myself, and she expresses optimism that my kids will do fine, and I gush on about how much we like it here so far.

"The McDonald's is nice," I say, racking my brain for something I know about this new town we're living in now. Or is that a Burger King?

"Oh, that's where all the drug addicts hang out," she says.

"Well, how nice for them!" I'm working hard, here.

She goes back to her typing while I start filling out the packet of papers required to get my kids into public school. I write my new address and phone number so many times that I finally memorize it. I sign my name, allowing my children to take buses to school, from school, and on field trips. I allow their likeness to be used on school materials. I promise not to sue the district if they get abrasions or contusions on the playground or in gym class. I swear that it's okay for Jack to have an inhaler and Caroline to take a Tylenol if she gets a headache. My signature is starting to look like that of a congressman or a rock star—a large cursive D and a squiggly line trailing it. After twenty minutes of filling in forms, I would give permission to have my children's school pictures put on kiddieporn.com if they would just take the papers away.

When I think I'm finished, I hand the stack to the secretary, and she starts flipping through the pages, checking my work. I'm getting anxious to get back home and start putting some plates away.

"Oh, you didn't put down the last emergency contact," she says to me, smiling and pushing the papers back to me.

"Well, I put down the first five," I say, "my home number, my cell phone number, my husband's work number, and his cell phone number, as well as his international business travel cell phone number. If you can't reach him in Germany and have him take care of whatever problem you have, well, good luck getting anyone else to do it!"

"We need a nonfamily member, like a neighbor or a friend, who we can call if we can't reach you or your husband," she says.

"Look, I don't have much of a life," I tell her. "I'm usually just at home, either sorting dirty clothes and eating Cheez-Its or sorting clean clothes and watching Law and Order reruns." I hadn't *planned to confide this last part to anyone here so soon, but so be it. "And if I do go anywhere, I have my cell phone. I really don't see the need to involve a nonfamily member."*

"We really need something filled in there," she insists.

I'm starting to get peeved. "Okay, the truth is I don't know anyone here yet. We just moved in a couple of days ago."

"You don't have a neighbor?" she asks in a sweet voice.

"Yes, of course I have a neighbor. I just don't know her yet. I haven't met her yet. I'm sure she's very nice and would eventually be willing to come and get Caroline or Jack if they should suffer a contusion on the playground, but right now I don't know anyone."

She just looks at me. We seem to be at a stalemate, and I've got those plates to put away.

"Okay, you know what," I say, "I know you. You seem nice. Why don't you put your name and number down there?"

She is staring at me, and she looks a little bit afraid.

"Go ahead! Your number is right there on the phone next to you. And your name is . . . ." I look at the nameplate on the front of her desk. " . . . Janet McLaughlin. Go ahead! You, Janet McLaughlin, can be my sixth line of defense against the school nurse having to handle something herself for a change. I've spent more time with you than I've spent with any person in this frickin' state. So I'm sorry, Janet, but you're going to just have to put your goddamn name and number down on this form!"

You would think that school guidance secretaries would be better prepared for the moving mother. Maybe by putting their desks behind bulletproof glass and speaking through an intercom. By the time we get to the day of registering our kids for school, we've been through hell and are not quite back. Knowing there are still dark days ahead, we're not in the best of moods.

Tip #28: The sooner you get your kids settled into school, the sooner they become someone else's guilt trip.

Getting your children settled into their new school is *the* top priority, numero uno, on the moving mom's list. If you can just get them into school, they'll start to meet kids and get into some kind of routine. They'll get loaded down with a bunch of homework and science fair projects, and then you can have a few hours free to get some things done.

This is not an easy task, especially if you're moving in the middle of the school year. I've read a lot of advice from moving experts with impressive letters after their names, and they say it's actually better for the kids if you move in the middle of the school year. They instantly have peers to surround them in school and they can stay busy. Moving in the summer, while easier on the mom, gives them too much free time in a place where they know no one. You'll never get the plates put away.

However, a mid-year move puts your child in the fearful and loathsome position of walking into school one day as The New Kid. It's up to you, Mom, to prepare your children using tactics of cheer, humor, and cash bribes.

I try to give my kids pep talks and downplay the drama. I let them buy outrageously expensive and trendy clothes, shoes with wheels, backpacks that talk—anything to make it easier for them. I even once told my kids as I was driving them to their new school that they should feel lucky.

"Think about how stressful this would be if you were really, really fat or had some kind of deformity," I said, cheerfully. They stared at me, their deer-in-the-headlights expression changing to one of horror.

I remind my kids that while the first day as The New Kid is terribly stressful, the second day as The New Kid is pretty sweet. By the second day, everyone in the school knows you came from an exotic location such as western Pennsylvania, and your strange, alien ways make you all the more appealing. You're a rock star on the second day. You're *Rebel Without a Cause.*

My kids are the most resilient I've ever known. They've gone into their first day of school overwhelmed with nail-biting worry, but come out on the other side happy, with a few new friends and a locker combination memorized. Moving so often has made Michael the king of adjustment in school, where he has had to learn three different styles of printing in three different schools before he learned cursive writing. That boy's fine motor skills are *fine.*

The kids' first few days of school are not my best work. I get so wrapped up in successfully getting them to school in one piece, I sometimes forget about getting them home. About five minutes before they're supposed to be walking in the front door from the bus, I remember I didn't tell them what bus they're supposed to ride home or what bus stop they're supposed to get off at. Then I run around the neighborhood looking for them, where they've inevitably gotten off at the wrong stop. When I finally find them, I have to hear a big lecture about how every house in our neighborhood looks alike and the streets all have similar names (this is true). It's after this first day of school that we stick an old Mondale for President campaign sign in our front yard. Our house stands out after that.

Michael once about gave me a heart attack when he didn't get off the bus on his first day at his new school in Illinois. I was sure he had been abducted by cigarette-smoking high school kids who surely hung around the elementary school, just looking for a confused-looking third grader unsure of which bus to get on. In actuality, Michael was sitting quietly in the back of the bus, politely waiting for the bus driver to tell him where to get off. She was parking her bus in the lot when she got the radio call from the school that "some kid's mother" wants to know where he is. She said she had to walk all the way to the back of the bus to find him, happily looking out the window. The whole time I was still on the phone, not exhaling, picturing what a bunch of high school sophomores could do to torment my little son.

At least with public schools, you just send your kids and wait for the fallout. Whenever we had a preschooler, I had to go the added mile of choosing which school was best suited to teaching my little one how not to eat paste, Play-Doh, or boogers. When Jack was three, I was told I couldn't get him into the Montessori School because he was too old.

"Most of our pupils start well before two," the woman lectured me on the phone.

Two? *Two?*

"Who are you kidding?" I snapped back at her. "That's not preschool; that's day care." I felt I had the right to be snippy; my three-year-old was just dealt his first big rejection.

When we moved to south Jersey, Caroline was four and had been in a nice Lutheran preschool. I was looking for something similar. You've got to hand it to the Lutherans for putting religion in a nice, neat perspective. Their under-zealousness was just what I was looking for. I couldn't find a preschool with "Lutheran" in the name, so I made the mistake of broadening my search to include "Christian."

One school was particularly excited about having me come to preview their preschool. I knew I was in trouble when the secretary told me she had arranged for me to meet the pastor-principal. I didn't want to meet the pastor-principal. Really, don't make me meet the pastor-principal. I'm just looking for a preschool where my daughter can say a quick prayer before her Ritz Bitz and juice, and maybe learn a couple verses of that Noah's Ark song.

But I met the pastor-principal. I had an interview with him, was given a three-ring binder of information about the school, and took an hour-long tour with him. He told me this wasn't just a preschool! This was a K through twelve Christian experience, where strong values were number one! It's all about Family!

I knew I had to manage an escape when the pastor-principal told me the school's Christian values follow the kids right home in their nonlogo backpacks. The children were not permitted to watch network TV while at home, nor were they allowed to listen to secular music.

"And that includes so called *Christian rock.*" The pastor-principal's fingers made big talon-like quotes in the air, and he said the last two words like they were the bane of the existence of all pastor-principals. I was guessing that Caroline's favorite music, the Smashing Pumpkins cassette she had swiped from Michael's room, wasn't going to make it here for show and tell. Nor would she be permitted to show up at school at all, given the dress code, which forbade pants for girls and any clothing that bore a logo, advertisement, visible brand name, product endorsement, or picture or word of any kind. I was searching for a preschool for a four-year-old girl who a) would not wear skirts or dresses or anything pink or purple. Ever. b) was going through a stage where she would only wear Jack's clothes—boys' athletic wear three sizes too big for her, and c) about every other day insisted on wearing her favorite outfit—Jack's black Allen Iverson jersey that came down past her knees and a backward baseball cap.

Caroline and this preschool was a match made in hell. I got out of the rest of the appointment by saying the magic words: "We're Catholic."

Tip #29: The faster you can join the kick line, the better.

When moving, I try very hard not to use the phrase, "We're not going to be able to participate because we just moved here." I make every attempt to jump right in and do everything that everyone else is doing. Tim says I "hit the ground running." Sometimes that means also stumbling, tripping, falling, and ending up on the bumper of someone's car. Eventually you learn to keep up.

Two days after our move into the house in Kentucky, Caroline came home from school, and after starting in on her homework, watching part of a TV show, and having a snack, turned to me casually and in between bites of a Pop Tart said, "I have a band concert tonight."

"You're in a band?" I asked.

"*School* band, Mother," she said. "Remember? I'm in band? I play clarinet?"

Yes, I remembered. We had just spent about $500 to buy the clarinet that we had been renting because it seemed easier to mail a check for that amount than to drive twelve miles to the instrument rental place to return the clarinet in the last few days before we moved. But those frantic days of not having a spare twenty minutes to run an errand were over; we were in the house, and I was finding some satisfaction in the fact that we were all under one roof, along with our stuff, such as it was.

"Did you say you have a concert *tonight*?"

"Yes, it's at seven, but I have to be there by six-twelve."

Okay, we can do this. I started mentally walking through the next hour. It's 5:15. I'll just throw on a pair of khakis, find a lipstick . . .

"And I need a black skirt and white blouse. And a pair of black dress shoes," Caroline casually added, popping the last bite of Tart into her mouth. "And I need a new reed."

There's nothing like an emergency school band concert to force you to find the closest JCPenney,

Payless, and music store. Of course, I wasn't aware of the shortcuts yet, so I was still driving through two counties to get to a mall that ended up being on the other side of my neighborhood. On the way to the music store, I discovered where the post office is, which was nice.

You won't be able to do everything, but try to do as much as possible without pushing yourself to the point of bursting into tears during patriotic songs at whatever concert you're attending.

Tip #30: Joining extra-curricular clubs, gangs, and cults will make your children happier.

After we have school tackled, we try to get involved in as much as possible as quickly as we can. Ever since we lived in Virginia, which was chock full of military families, I learned from the pros how to make friends fast.

At a library story hour I had taken Michael to, a lady walked up to me and asked, "Do you want to get the kids together sometime?"

"Do I know you?" I asked suspiciously. Up until that time, I had worked full-time and relegated talk like this to our babysitter.

"No, but you will once we get the kids together," she said, jotting down her name and address on a piece of paper. Her husband was military, she only had three years to make friends and have some kind of fulfilling life before she had to leave and start over again. I learned valuable lessons from her and other moms there. I've started playgroups with people who said later, "Why didn't we ever do this before?" Because you didn't have a raving maniac of a moving mother in your neighborhood before, that's why. We're on a time line here, so either get on board or stay out of our way.

I found that scouts were the perfect sized group for my children to make friends fast in a new town. Michael liked Cub Scouts a lot. Despite the pacifist that he is, he liked shooting BB guns, archery, crafts involving knives, and maniacal survivalist skills like learning how to build a shelter out of bark, snow, and litter.

My kids thrived in scouts, playgroups, sports, music, and a cornucopia of lessons of every kind. They've had to learn so many different styles of piano, with each of their teachers adamant that her way is right, that they could probably play with their elbows. Like me, they've become very good at adapting, adjusting, and moving forward, one step at a time.

Tip #31: Don't let the natives' weird ways put you off.

Wherever you turn, you're going to find people doing things differently, not at all the way you did it where you used to live, and just plain wrong. Get used to it. They're not going to change, even though your old way is so obviously better. You're going to have to adapt to the new way.

My family and I have learned that in some towns, the Pinewood Derby is a fun project where boys can learn a handicraft and discover the spirit of teamwork and competition. And in other towns it's a death match between dads who work as engineers for Hoover versus dads who worked as engineers for Goodyear.

After pulling together Michael's Pinewood Derby car, we ended up at such a race, so far out of our league it was scary. I showed up with a chip on my shoulder (not a real chip, but almost. In an attempt to carve the block of wood into something that resembled a car-like shape, I had stabbed myself in the palm with an Exacto knife, so I showed up at the Derby bandaged and well on my way to stigmata, not to mention really ticked off because there was green oil-based paint on my kitchen counter). Michael's car was made to look like Tommy, the Green Power Ranger, with glitter slathered on and a quarter taped to the top, to make it roughly the weight it was supposed to be. At his old Cub Scout pack, Michael's car would have been awesome. Here, it was a green, sparkly piece of crap.

By the time the Green Ranger car wobbled up to the finish line, the winner's dad had already taken his car off the track and was fine-tuning it for the finals, using a set of tools that looked like McCoy's surgical instruments on *Star Trek*.

We learned that in some towns First Communion is a spiritual sacrament of initiation where young people are welcomed into the fulfillment of the Holy Eucharist. And in some towns it's a reason to have a girls size seven white wedding gown professionally altered, get out the booster seat at the hair salon, have your child photographed in twelve different solemn poses of prayer, and throw a catered party for eighty.

The high school homecoming dance, in some towns, is an affair in the school gym, decorated with balloons and crepe paper, where the boy's mom picks up the girl and drops them off and then picks them up three hours later and takes them to Pizza Hut. In other towns, homecoming means floor-length gowns, limos, $50 up-dos, corsages, and photo ops.

In some towns, eighth grade graduation is an assembly in the cafetorium-auditeria with certificates, gold stickers, boys with their shirts tucked in and girls in nylons. In other towns, graduating from eighth grade means caps and gowns, processionals, seating charts, speeches, a lot of pomp, and even more circumstance.

We tried to keep up. I started taking neighbors up on their offers of "If you need anything or have any questions, call me." I would pick an afternoon when I had a few hours and call one of the numbers, reading a litany of questions. Am I supposed to buy my kids' teachers gifts at the end of the year? How much should I spend? For my kids' birthday parties, how elaborate should the goody bags be? Do the parents stay for baseball practice, or do people here just drop their kids and run?

The form that I just signed, promising not to use curse words at my son's soccer game, does that mean when I'm speaking to the kids, or does it also include when I'm yelling at the ref?

We tried to cover all bases by doing everything possible, hoping that the regionally appropriate thing would pop out and be the only thing noticed. Knowing people take communion differently in every parish, Jack started a little routine that looked like an autistic baseball pitcher—bowing, touching his forehead, chest, shoulders, stomach and nose in a pre-communion sign of the cross unlike anything the poor, confused priest had ever seen.

The end result is that we sometimes just have to shrug and admit that we didn't know any better. Caroline has been the only girl at the piano recital who didn't get a bouquet of flowers from her parents. She just looked at me, and we simultaneously gave each other that "Who knew?" look. It wasn't that I was stupid; I just didn't know the local customs. I felt like it would have been easier to just hang a sign around our necks that said "WE ARE FROM SOMALIA" and leave it at that.

Despite your worst fears, your children probably will pick up a few regionalisms along the way, but only the ones that annoy you the most. Michael pronounces the word water "wood-er" because we let him live in south Jersey for a few years. Caroline drinks "soda" instead of our pop, and Jack wears "sneakers" instead of the tennis shoes that we bought him. You know your children have become East Coasters when they go "down the shore," carry a "pocketbook," and say the word "yeah" with a short *i* vowel sound.

One part of you will want to stay true to your roots and insist that they keep talking like they're from the native land, but actually it's your native land, not theirs. If you move as often as we do, your kids will be interstate vagabonds. And it's a losing battle anyway. If you're lucky, you'll eventually move back to someplace where you once fit in.

Accents are something that eventually grow on you. Before I moved to north Jersey I stood in line at the Statue of Liberty for two hours behind a sixty-year-old woman with the most obnoxious Brooklyn accent I've ever heard. Then I moved there, and listening to that accent every single day didn't bother me. Our Midwestern accent, however, bothered them.

"Are you from the South?" they would ask us. Then, when we lived in the South, we are told our northern axints were sooo griiiite.

CHAPTER 10

I Rode that Welcome Wagon Like It Was a Stallion

Getting Yourself Settled in Your New Home

Number 127. Call number 127. Call. Number. One. Hundred. And. Twen. Tee. Se. Ven.

I'm sitting in the New Jersey Department of Motor Vehicles in a gray molded plastic chair for the third consecutive hour, waiting to get my car registered here. In my left hand I'm squeezing a little piece of paper that says 127, which is now a sweat-soaked piece of pulp, looking like it went through a warm wash cycle. In my right hand I'm holding a manila folder with documents that chronicle my history and the complete life of my car. Also I brought my baby book. The DMV requires so many documents to prove that I am who I claim to be, I figured rather than bring the bare minimum—my birth certificate, marriage certificate, social security documentation, proof of residency, proof of citizenship, and my most recent utility bill—I would play it safe and bring along a lock of my baby hair and my first kindergarten finger painting. It couldn't hurt.

Sitting here is making me relate to how my great-grandmother must've felt coming through Ellis Island. There are people who have been here so long they need a shave. Babies are crying, and one obviously needs a diaper change. People are speaking in foreign languages, older people are starting to lie down on the floor, and the guy next to me has his head on my shoulder. And I have stopped caring.

Just puh-leeeeze call number 127!

I've had about three hours to think and have decided that this is the original House of Pain, *the place where the concept of frustration was created and where it is even now being tweaked and perfected in a back room.*

Then they call number 127. I jump up like I'm on The Price is Right. *The guy next to me slides off my shoulder and slumps onto my chair. He might be dead. I approach the open window and smile like an idiot at the woman behind the counter. My heart is beating fast. I am so grateful that I'm finally up to this window, that I've been called, that I feel a little Stockholm syndrome sweep over me. I'll do anything for this woman, I'm so grateful that she called my number, and so hopeful that she'll give me those yellow plates for my car. I will hold a machine gun at a bank robbery for you, I telepathically tell her. I will be your Patty Hearst.*

Ten minutes later, I'm still at the window trying to figure out what went wrong. The problem seems to be the fact that I've done this wacky, madcap thing called moving to the state of New Jersey and bringing my car with me. She's telling me I need proof of insurance before I can get plates. My new insurance agent, Stan, has already told me I can't get New Jersey insurance until I have a car registered in New Jersey.

"Think about it," Stan had said to me. "How can we give your car New Jersey insurance if it's not even a New Jersey car yet?" This clearly is a pickle, especially since Stan has made my car seem like it has a personality of its own, with feelings and citizenship issues. I'm inclined to believe the woman behind this counter, though, since she's wearing what appears to be a prison guard's uniform. But I'm not leaving spot 127 until I get some plates, so I keep insisting that Stan has refused to give me insurance until I get the plates.

"Surely, this isn't the first time this has come up," I say to her. "Am I the first car owner who has ever moved into this state?" I say it nicely, though. I do not want to tick this woman off, for any reason. She holds the key to my freedom.

After some more conversation and maybe some intervention by a supervisor (I'm not sure. It gets blurry, and I may have even blacked out from the fear), I end up with the plates. How did that happen? I think she had just been messing with me. The prison guards at DMV have perfected that. They like to see you almost wet your pants with anxiety and then throw you a bone so they can move onto their next victim: Number 128.

Tip #32: Moving your car can be complicated. Abandoning it in a bad neighborhood before your move should be at least considered.

How do you describe the holy mess of getting a new license and car registration to someone who has always lived in the same state? Remember when you were sixteen and taking that driver's test? Or when you bought your first car? You thought things went so badly because you were young and inexperienced? No, things went to hell because the people running the motor vehicle branch of government are evil sadists of cult-like proportions. They are underpaid, working in an office that reeks of dirty diapers, forced to wear polyester uniforms the color of sick, and they've chosen to take out their whiny gripes on us. The post office with its occasional berserk employee has nothing on the DMV, where the workers are saving up their strength to one day take over the world. Whoever is at the counter at the time will help them by holding the machine guns.

Seven of our moves were out of state and required new plates, new driver's licenses, different insurance, and dozens of inspections. Twice I had to take a written driver's test, which inexplicably gets harder to pass as you get older and have more miles on you. When I was sixteen and had only been driving for a few weeks, I passed the Ohio driver's test with flying colors. When I was thirty-six and had to take the Illinois test, I know I didn't do well, but the girl behind the counter was very young and I think she felt sorry for me. I filled in the little circles with my number two pencil, sitting sideways at a desk built for an ten-year-old with an eating disorder, while holding onto the back of Caroline's shirt as she ran tethered and spinning, flinging an arc of Cheerios and droplets of Juicy Juice. The girl looked at my completed test and said, "You passed." With a look of pity, she wrote *A* and put a little smiley face on the top and then slid it right into the trashcan at her feet.

Then when I was forty, I took the test in New Jersey, where by that time even Hell had computers, and the DMV used a high-tech computerized driver's test. No cheating allowed, no sympathy A's and certainly no smiley faces. I had seen the way people in New Jersey drive and was confident that I could pass any test they gave me. I had been driving for twenty-four years and had committed hardly any serious car crimes. How hard could it be? I knew when to turn, when to stop, and I even had successfully parallel parked once in the past ten years. So I leafed through the booklet at the red lights on my way to take the test.

It was forty questions, each one automatically popping up on the computer screen in its turn. Your total number of wrong answers showed up on the top right corner of the screen, so you could keep a running tab of how miserable you were doing. You were only allowed to miss three questions. If you got four wrong, you failed and a big red *X* flashed on your screen, a frown face showed up in the corner, buzzers sounded, and the trolls in the back room danced around their fire and roared with glee.

I was doing all right at first. What does an eight-sided sign mean? A) Yield B) Caution C) Stop. This was a piece of cake!

Around question ten, they started to get harder. What would be a reason for approaching a sharp curve slowly? A) To save wear and tear on your tires, B) To be able to take in the scenery, C) To be able to stop if someone is in the roadway. Since there was no "all of the above" I had to think about this one. I could see the scenery advantage but didn't think the DMV gave a rat's ass about my view while driving. And choice *C* was stupid—what if someone wasn't in the roadway? That seems like a single-case scenario to me, and that should be another question altogether. Wear and tear on tires? This test was supposed to be about safe driving, not taking care of your car. Are we going to have to answer questions about how to properly clean out the glove box, too?

Then they started to get just plain bizarre. You needn't stop your vehicle for a frozen dessert truck when A) it shows flashing red lights, B) it shows a stop signal arm, C) a person is crossing the roadway to or from the frozen dessert truck, D) on a dual highway if you're on the other side of a safety island or median from the frozen dessert truck. Okay, that's just ridiculous. The ice cream man now gets his own question. Who is making up these tests?

By the time I got to question thirty, I was in trouble. I had already gotten two wrong and I had skipped one question—A five-ounce glass of wine contains the same amount of alcohol as: A) one pint of whiskey B) a gallon of wine C) a six-pack of beer D) one twelve-ounce can of beer. I knew *B* wasn't right, but I was having a mental block trying to picture what a pint was. I couldn't stop myself from thinking about a gallon milk jug full of red wine, and my stomach was turning over slightly. I'd get back to that one later.

When I had gotten as far as question thirty-nine, I was in a full sweat, feeling dizzy, and looking around for a paper bag to breathe into. I had used up my three wrong answers and had skipped questions concerning how deep my tire treads had to be *(A) 3/8 inch B) 3/16 inch C) 2/32 inch D) 4/10 inch)* and what the penalty was for a third offense for DUI. These were things I hadn't studied in the book, thinking I would have to be an idiot to ever get to a third DUI offense and confident that one of the six inspections I had to have done to my car every twelve months would surely alert me to a possible tire tread infraction.

I was starting to get the evil eye from the lady in the throw-up-colored shirt. I had been in there so long they were getting ready to close. I shut my eyes, held my breath, and hit some buttons, guessing on the answers. A big green exclamation point flashed on my screen. I passed! I hugged all the prison guards, posed for my picture and got my New Jersey license. Another state conquered.

Tip #33: Don't expect your mother's Welcome Wagon.

Remember Welcome Wagon? Ladies in knee-length skirts and sensible shoes would come over and sit on your cardboard boxes with you and give you refrigerator magnets and jar-opening gripper discs from the local shoe store and meat market. Yeah, they don't do that anymore. Those ladies have better things to do with their time—especially now that Pinterest has been invented—and frankly, so do you. A twenty-first century move isn't going to get anywhere with coupons and giveaways.

I have vague memories of the Welcome Wagon lady sitting with me shortly after one of my early moves, pulling coupons out of her tote bag one by one, touting all the local merchants. I politely oohed and ahhed over the complimentary potato chip bag clip. I actually did intend to take advantage of the buy-one-gallon-of-paint-get-30 percent-off-the-second-gallon, and thought I'd get a pet groomed. All of the coupons, free stuff—the entire tote bag and its contents—got shoved into the junk drawer never to be thought of again.

My point is, don't mourn the Welcome Wagon lady. You'll do fine without her. Today's Welcome Wagon consists of a team of new neighbors, the secretary at your kids' school, the soccer coach's wife (or husband), the guy who cuts your hair, and the girl who sweeps up your hair at the salon that you stumble upon in desperation when you can't find the hair ties, and you feel the onset of dreadlocks.

Tip #34: Prioritize your list of adjustments, from bad to oh-my-freaking-gosh-are-you-serious.

Emotionally, it may be harder for kids to get settled in, but at least their adjustments are centered on friend-making opportunities, fitting in, and having fun. You can gauge how well the kids are getting settled by how often they smile. As adults, our adjustment is based on boring things that give you a headache. The more things you accomplish, the more miserable you are. Our adjustment is measured by how often we cry and/or assault strangers.

The good news is you will smile again. That's how you know you're done settling in.

Making friends is not quite a priority. It's really quite difficult to make new friends when you're old and at least temporarily unattractive. In some of my neighborhoods, pleasant women will come over with a bundt cake. You know you deserve that bundt cake. Unfortunately, when they show up at my door is about the time that I'm wading through rooms full of junk, and personal hygiene is taking a backseat. I'm usually in the middle of sorting pieces of the disassembled dog crate and the weight machine, which have once again been mixed together and which I've reassembled into something that looks like an S&M apparatus with comfortable padded edges. I have my bad hair clamped by my daughter's American Girl doll's hair clip, like a tiny lavender sparkly Jaws of Life. I free myself from the dog crate-weighted-death machine to answer the door. I watch the bundt cake neighbor sprint down the sidewalk and I never see her again.

I've learned to use the word "friend" very loosely and very quickly. Tim and I were in front of our new house, trying to figure out how to get an old hockey puck out of a prickly bush without a trip to the emergency room, when our new across-the-street neighbor came out.

"That lady has the weirdest color hair," Tim said.

"That's not a very nice thing to say about my best friend," I shot back.

"Oh, she's your best friend? Really? Then what's her name?"

"I don't know," I say defensively. "Sherry or Sheila or something that starts with an Sh or a D. It's Denise. Darla. Shelly . . . " I start to raise my voice, seeing if she'll turn when I hit the right name. It's not until I yell, "Hey, you with the purple hair!" that she looks at me.

"See?" I tell Tim as I wave to Purple Hair. "She and I are buds."

In some of my new neighborhoods, I've stooped so low as to allow the Mary Kay Cosmetics lady to come to my house to do the free makeover they offer to people whose names are in the real estate transactions. Mary Kay is the modern-day version of the Welcome Wagon. If you've recently moved in, she will find you. In return for your free gift—a sample lipstick the size of a pushpin in a shade they can't sell in the regular tubes—you'll sit through a ninety-minute lecture and demonstration that will make you wonder how you've managed to live with that dried up old prune of a face all these years.

"Could you please not bring the big pink Cadillac?" I would ask my Mary Kay representative when she would call. "I want my neighbors to think I have a real friend coming over."

At times I've been forced to join groups I have no business being in, just because it's a group of ready-made female adults I can hang out with. Once, I decided to give Le Leche League a try. I reasoned that since we all breastfed our babies, I was sure to have something in common with these women. Lesson learned: I don't have anything in common with those women. Some of us were more fervent about breastfeeding than others of us. I knew I was in trouble at our first meeting when I pulled out a bottle to feed Caroline and the temperature in the room dropped twenty degrees. I was at least glad that two-year-old Jack would have some kids to play with. Some of them were a little older by a couple of years, but this would be nice for him and maybe he'd make some new friends. Then it was snack time and those kids came running in, unbuttoned their mothers' blouses, and latched on. I was shocked, but Jack was downright traumatized. He let out an ear-splitting scream, unable to take his eyes off a five-year-old nursing while solving a Rubic's Cube. I grabbed my contraband formula bottle, diaper bag, baby, and toddler and fled. Cross those earth mamas off my list of potential friends.

Face it. Friend-making is not even going to make the to-do list right after a move. We have a huge number of things to do, some of them car related, legally required and scary. Sharing PMS stories and swapping recipes aren't high on the list. Or even on the list. Which brings us to . . .

Tip #35: Make your moving list a work of art, and then burn it in ritualistic flames.

My moving list is immense. I always swear I'm going to keep it to use the next time, so I won't forget anything, but you can't keep a document like that. It is normally about six typed pages, double-spaced. It has notes in the margins with things like "original birth certificate only!!!!!" and "Proof of rabies shot????" And then there are some weak ink marks where I've obviously fallen asleep with the pen in my hand. When I look at the list, I have memories of a weariness that has no name, and I have to destroy it, or I'd never move again. Like childbirth, we must forget the pain to keep the process going.

Some of the items on the list are short and sweet: "Register to vote" requires a phone call and one trip. Others are so involved they take on a life of their own. Anything that starts with "Deal with . . . " is a bad sign. Also anything with the words "out-of-state" or "insurance" or "car." When tackling "Deal with issue of Michael's out-of-state car insurance," I have to put on sweats, drape a towel around my neck, and mix myself a super-sized Bloody Mary.

If your moving company gives you a suggested checklist, toss that thing. It's useless. One that I was given had three things listed under what to do three weeks before your move. Count 'em—three things. If I were stupid enough to believe that, I would have thought I still had time to take daily showers and return the clarinet. One item listed on every week is "Contact your moving counselor to review and confirm all arrangements for your move." That part is true. You'll have to call that lady every week to make sure you're on. Otherwise, you'll be left out on your front lawn with a suitcase and forgotten like an orphan.

Here are some suggestions for your Moving List. In addition to the obvious items, I think you're going to want these covered:

- Locate a Girl Scout. Get cookie order in ASAP.
- Call kids' old school. Send check for $55 for postage to mail yearbooks to the kids (extra $20 for fake signatures of their friends).
- Cruise high school parking lot for potential babysitters.

- Order a bunch of stuff from catalogs, so quality and quantity of junk mail will improve.
- Call buyers of our old house. Make mouse squeaky noises and hang up. Laugh.
- Go to the mall and stalk people with good haircuts. Demand name and number of their salon.
- Find an orthodontist, and get the kids some braces. Really, this time actually do it. And quickly, before you have to move again.
- Buy and fill out pretty Change of Address cards. Spend hours addressing them to all your friends. Leave them on cluttered desk and forget to mail them.

And last but not least:

- Be nice to someone, so she'll be your friend. Otherwise, there'll be no bundt cake for you.

CHAPTER 11

So *This* Is What They Meant by " . . . Or Worse"

Can This Marriage Survive a Move?

I take a deep breath and look over at Tim, his hands gripping the steering wheel. He slowly puts the car in park and turns off the engine.

"Okay, move out," he says. We exit the car at the same time and walk briskly to the double doors. We're at Haverty's Furniture, the fourth stop on today's furniture tour. We've been shopping for the past four weekends and haven't

bought a thing. And we have a lot to buy. Once again we've moved into a house where our formerly decent furniture looks like crap. We're in a traditional house with contemporary furniture, the same furniture that we bought because we had moved into a contemporary house, and our traditional furniture looked like crap.

This cycle might be exciting for a normal couple. Buying new things can be fun. But not when you're married to someone with Tim's shopping philosophy. He doesn't just hate furniture salesmen, he views them as the Lex Luthors of retail. They are to be destroyed, but not before being humiliated and exposed, and after a dramatic parking-garage chase scene, a sword fight, and letters to supervisors.

We walk through the doors, and Tim stage whispers something to me out of the side of his mouth. I can't understand him, but I see what I'm guessing is the general topic. There's a guy in a suit right inside the door, hidden behind a fake Roman column with a big beige vase on it that holds big spiky, pointy things.

"Hi, folks!" The guy comes jumping out with his business card extended. "How are y'all?"

"Gahh!" I'm startled. Tim has vanished. Like some kind of X Man, he has maneuvered an early escape. Before the salesman can ask me if I need help finding the particular piece of furniture I'm here to put on a high-interest payment plan, I quickly begin one of my tactics.

"We're only looking today. We're not really focused on too much, just the nineteen downstairs rooms. That vase of spikes would actually look great in our conservatory," I tell him, smiling. "We don't have enough decorative things that could put your eye out."

He smiles back, and I swear I see his pupils dilate and fangs begin to emerge.

"Well, if you need help, I'm Carl," he says, handing me another business card. I'm stuffing them into my purse, giving them a good crinkle so I'll remember later to toss them. "Take your time and just to let ya know, everything with the red tag is fifty percent off, everything with the green sticker is thirty days same as cash, refund, finance, in-stock, delivery, fabric samples, custom, sale, one-day-only . . . "

I hear random familiar furniture store vocabulary words all strung together, and I know not to bother trying to understand any of it. I couldn't be less interested if there were verbs included. Yet I continue to smile and nod, using up the time I need.

About twenty minutes later, after my spiel on my "conservatory" in which I make a sketch drawing of the south wing, I leave Carl and find Tim refilling his coffee cup in the customer appreciation center near the kitchen hutches.

"Did you hear me when we first came in?" he says. "I whispered, 'This is the place that has the cookies and coffee!' Remember? This is the store we came to three Saturdays ago!" Tim is looking around, making sure no one is sneaking up on us.

"Nice escape, by the way. The guy was so eager to pin me down, I was nearly harpooned by a spiky thing and knocked cold by a Roman column." I tell him. "Oh, and by the way. I think I want a conservatory."

Tim just shakes this off. "Do you want to know what I found or what?"

"Yes, do tell."

"No black and cream weaves in the fabric samples, but style-wise they've got the chair and *loveseat we've been looking for. Forget tables, they're made out of paperboard. This place is still on the B list for the dining room, but shows some early promise for the living room.*

"What about rugs?"

Tim snorts. "Don't even say that word in here."

"His name's Carl, by the way," I tell Tim, grabbing a fistful of cookies. "He favors his left foot slightly. I think you can take him."

Furniture shopping with Tim is like playing spy with my grade-school girlfriends. Usually I'm sacrificed early on so Tim can fulfill the mission unbothered by the salesman and his henchmen. I've learned lots of tricks to keep salesmen busy. Sometimes I talk about the huge mansion I just moved into. Sometimes I speak in foreign accents ("how you say, enter-tain-ment cen-ter") or really slowly like I've had a stroke.

One time Tim and I reversed roles, with disastrous results. Tim was unprepared and ran out of things to say to the salesman, got frustrated and impatient, and ended up in an argument and threatening to call the manager. Meanwhile, I was too slow to be the main spy and was power walking in figure eights, trapped in a maze of desks when I heard Tim's faraway voice yelling across the showroom, "Abort! Abort!"

How we ever end up with anything decent to sit, lie, or lean on is beyond me.

Tip #36: Adapting to the new house is going to require some creative financing and hours of HGTV.

You may not realize it when you first see the house, or when you do the final walk-through. Or when you walk into its emptiness before the moving truck arrives. But when you start to put your furniture in your new house, some problems are sure to arise.

Every one of our moves has left us with at least a couple rooms full of furniture that simply doesn't work. A set of flowered wingback chairs in a ski lodge house; framed pictures that won't fit on any single wall unless they're hung sideways; a seven-piece bedroom set for a kid whose room is now the size of a bank vault.

Our houses are always works in progress, so we're either waiting for drapes to come in, rugs to go on sale, or time on a weekend to attack furniture stores. By the time we finally pull the house together, it's time to sell it and move again. Invariably we end up moving into a house where those things we just purchased don't fit.

When people come to see our new houses, we greet them at the door with a litany of disclaimers: "Hi! Come on in! How was your drive? There aren't enough pictures up, we did not pick this wallpaper, window treatments are on order, we're aware that the family room furniture looks like shit in this house, and please just squint when you go upstairs."

So Tim and I have become experts on furniture shopping. We know the pros and cons of large chains versus mom-and-pop stores. We know how to use our time wisely, how to divide and conquer. And we know where the cookies are.

Once we tried a different furniture shopping plan: I went out on reconnaissance missions to scout out potential purchases, but by myself I was no match for the Carls of this world. After hours of badgering and coercion, I caved and came home with a delivery scheduled for a king-sized mattress for a bed we don't own and a magenta sectional massage sofa with built-in refrigerator and electric hot plate.

"It seemed like the smart thing to do at the time," I said to Tim afterward. I had to follow up with a visit to a lawyer. And I had to return the free Arthur Murray dance lesson.

So Tim and I have fallen into a comfortable groove that only nine moves and thirty years of marriage can bring. We know each other's strengths and weaknesses, and now we know the same of every shift of furniture salesmen in seven states.

If you're new at this moving stuff, my advice to you is to look at this stage as the final challenge. If you're in the new house and you're starting to look around at what you've got and you're still married, congratulations! Your marriage has made it through a major hellish milestone. There's just one more thing you'll be asked to do. Now get in the car and pick out some furniture together! Carl is waiting, and if you're lucky, there will be cookies.

Tip #37: When buying new home furnishings, let Goodwill be the big winner.

Unless you have a lot of extra space for every piece of furniture you bring into your house, you're going to have to get rid of something ugly. This is harder than it first appears and may be a chink in the armor that is your marriage. To throw away or give away? If you and your husband agree on the answer to this question, brava. You're better off than I am.

This is an issue that never came up in the pre-Cana counseling that the Catholic Church sent us to. (That would be the pre-marriage counseling in which the priest told Tim to be "nice, like you are," told me to not let the dishes build up in the sink, and told us both to never take separate vacations. "I don't want to hear about Diane going to Hawaii with her girlfriends and Tim going to North Carolina with the guys," he told us. I'm ever so pleased to report that the Hawaiian opportunity has not happened yet. The dishes in the sink are another story.)

While we're compatible on buying new furniture, Tim and I are the opposite when it comes to getting rid of the things we can't use anymore. I feel sorry for them. I've given them first names and bios, and therefore I feel some compassion for their plight. Whitney, the crib that we used for all three of our children, had its own photo album.

On the other hand, Tim is like the guy who runs the greyhound track: Once something's usefulness is exhausted, kill it.

Tim is a big believer in the garbage. It bothers him when I find good homes for our things as opposed to throwing them in the trash. He thinks it's silly to cart things to Goodwill or the Salvation Army. He prefers the enema-clean feeling that only the landfill can offer.

In the early days of our marriage, when we were just starting to have enough money to replace the first hand-me-down furniture we'd been given, Tim told me that if you put a sofa on the curb on garbage day, the garbage men will pick it up and take it to a farm. I believed him. After all, a lot of our dog's puppies went to that farm when I was a little girl. I pictured our big couch full of romping and napping little mutts.

So that's why I agreed to put Eleanor, the big blue couch, on the curb. She was great, but she hadn't aged well. She was an Ethan Allen creation back in the Early American motif days of the 1970s. Bright blue chrysanthemums on an apple juice beige background; wooden arms with eagles carved into them; God-knows-what sticky substances encrusted into those carvings.

Still, I felt bad for her, seeing her sitting at the curb all sad, with stuff that stunk. I sat at the window all morning, watching, until the BFI truck arrived. The guy jumped off the back of the truck, eyed her up and down, lifted up the cushions, set them back down (I thought he was fluffing them), and then motioned to his buddy. Together they lifted Eleanor and heaved her into the back of what looked an awful lot like a regular garbage truck. *Uh-oh. This can't be right.* I started to rise up out of my chair.

Five minutes later, I picked myself up off the floor and called Tim at work.

"Find a good home, my *ass!*" I sobbed to Tim on the phone. "They crushed her! Right in front of me! All her bones broke, and now she's *dead!*"

Tim tried to salvage what had been a good scam up until now. He didn't want to screw up a future of furniture mass murder.

"Oh, there must've been a mix-up," he said. "I'm sure I told the guy on the phone we wanted the couch taken to the (inaudible words mumbled . . . *cough!*) They must've sent the wrong truck."

I was far cleverer for my next big disposal, a brown recliner that we had managed to hold onto for thirteen years, partly because the color hid all things that come out of the human body, all beverages, and most foods, except for the bright purple ones. By that time we were living in south Jersey, and we were on the trash pickers' main line. Starting the night before garbage pickup day, you could set anything at the curb, and pickup trucks would cruise by during the night, and by morning your things had disappeared. I was competing with our neighbors' junk and started displaying our things on tables with cloth-covered tiers and spotlights on the good stuff. Until they took the spotlights and tablecloths.

So that's where I set the brown chair, with only a little reluctance. I loved Brownie, but he had seen better days. A big, sharp thing was sticking out of his back and had already puncture-wounded our friend's son. The reclining action was broken, and we were all too afraid to pull the lever since the day Caroline was catapulted into a backward somersault, in the closest thing to a James Bond movie reenactment her brothers had ever seen. (It was awesome.)

Even though it still held strong memories for me—of snuggling all three of my toddlers, reading *Harold and the Purple Crayon*, and finding the complete set of Wizard of Oz figurines in its bowels—I finally agreed with Tim that it was time to put Brownie out to pasture. Even I had to admit, he was getting a little cranky in his old age. The chair, that is.

Garbage day morning I looked out and was shocked to see Brownie still at the curb. Not one trash picker had chosen him! With only minutes before the BFI crushmeister was due to come by on its death cruise, I ran out in my pajamas and dragged him behind a tree. Even then, I knew I was creating a serious problem down the line. If Tim came home from work and found the chair behind our front tree, he was going to have a fit. Despite the fact that he was brown, my attempts to camouflage Brownie with branches and leaves were futile. I had about nine hours to find a home for a hazardous, old recliner.

When the kids came home from school they were thrilled. Their dreams of white-trash glory had come true! Their parents had finally come to their senses and were seeing the advantage of outfitting the front lawn with upholstered furniture! Michael dragged it to the center of the yard and was holding a story hour with some little kids. Teenagers from other neighborhoods were starting to gather. Some skinhead with a pierced lip was curled up on it watching a street hockey game when I came out and shooed everyone away. What was the matter with those trash pickers?! This thing was clearly of high value. Look how popular it is out here! Why couldn't they see it?

Thirty minutes before Tim was due home from work, I was desperate enough to go next door and ask my friend Gail for help. Gail was an interior decorator who did things in a big way. When we first moved to the neighborhood, we thought she was a carpenter or a welder. Every time we saw her she was wearing safety goggles and operating one of the three pieces of power equipment she kept in her garage. When Gail heard that a client wanted a theme bedroom for a little boy, she would start by carving a bed frame out of a tree trunk.

I went to Gail because I half thought she would take Brownie and forge him into a lamp stand or something. She wasn't interested, but she did help me heave the thing up into the back of my van. I then started driving it around—where to I didn't know exactly. I just knew I had to get it off our property by the time Tim got home. It was raining and getting dark when I pulled up to Goodwill. It was closed. I pulled up to the back, where the sign said, "Do Not Leave Donated Items When Attendant Is Not on Duty." Getting big, old Brownie out of my van without Gail's help was a feat. I couldn't lift him, so I did a combination of pulling out and pushing from inside the van until he teetered on the edge. Then I gave a big shove and he crashed to the ground, on his side. I dragged him over near a sad little bike that someone else had left (hopefully, for the bike's sake, under better circumstances than this), and I drove away. When I last saw him, Brownie was standing in the rain. I choked back sobs all the way home.

When Tim got home from work that night, he said, "Hey, the brown chair is gone! All right!" I made a mental note to pack his lunch in the pink breast cancer awareness bag tomorrow. That one's for you, Brownie.

Tip #38: During a move, focus on your marriage's strengths, and try to avoid one another as much as possible.

No matter how compatible you are with another member of the human race, no matter what level of soul-mate bonding you've managed to achieve, you're not going to survive a move without at least one major area of contention.

Tim and I have worked out a nice arrangement on choosing houses (we hold campaigns and elections), moving day (we try to arrange to be in different geographic locations), and who is the designated driver at our going away parties (we alternate). Our downfall is setting up housekeeping in the new place. No matter how big our house is, I can't get Tim to agree that I should use the extra space to store stuff we don't use. He can't understand why I need a kitchen cabinet dedicated to dishes we haven't eaten off of in ten years, floor space in our closet for shoes I never wear, and a really large basement storage area for everything else we don't need anymore.

I don't dare leave Tim home alone during a garbage pick-up period. My trips away without him are carefully scheduled for no more than six consecutive days, ending before the next garbage day. Otherwise, Tim would use every minute I was gone to go through our things and throw away what we haven't used in the past few years. When I'm gone, he dusts and sweeps with a leaf blower. If it's not heavy enough to stay indoors, it doesn't deserve to live here. This house is not for the weak.

Some men couldn't give a hoot about what their house looks like. These are men whose wives are allowed to paint walls pink, hang antique hats in the hallway, and take their Precious Moments figurines out of their boxes. These women are allowed to have fluffy beds with lacy pillows, Victorian fainting couches, and Christmas trees decorated with burgundy bows.

These women are not even in the same species as me. I haven't been able to choose paint colors in two entire pie pieces of the color wheel because I'm married to a guy who claims he's *been* in touch with his feminine side, and she's got a crew cut.

I envy women who can go to a wallpaper store and put little bookmarks in the pages they like, review their choices, make a final decision, and place their order, all in the same day. I have to lug the eight maximum books home, lay them out for Tim and listen as he shoots down every one of my ideas.

"Too red, too big, too boring, not kitcheny enough, too blech, hate it, hate it, don't like plaid," he says, pointing to each one down the line. I take the whole mess back to the store and start all over with another eight ideas, any of which would be fine with me. I'm pretty easy to please. As long as it's not truly ugly, any wallpaper, paint, or decorating choice of any kind is really just fine. In fact, I'm almost un-female in that respect. Maybe my inner female side has a crew cut too, and that's why Tim and I have such a successful marriage.

It's interesting to see Tim interact with professionals. He's much more likely to trust their judgment over mine. When our friend Gail did some decorating work for us, Tim would patiently listen to her suggestions, look at the collage of paint cards, fabric samples, and wallpaper swatches she had spread on the floor, and then say, "Fine, whatever. But no ducks. And no plaid. Plaid blows."

Once, we decided to hire a faux painter to do some swishy paint job in a powder room. She was very artsy and exotic, and when she came into our house it was like Eastern Europe had exploded, and we were getting some of the fallout. I was fascinated that Tim would let a woman who looked and talked like a Bond girl go manic on our walls. I suspect she body painted some parts of the room. As it turned out, Tim was fine with it.

He was not so fine with the window treatment ladies. We've had four different decorators from JC Penney, one from a private designer, and several from Krissy's Kustom Kurtains or the equivalent. I can't say that there was much of a difference between the valance that Krissy stitched up on her Singer at her kitchen table, and the Roman shades custom designed by Paris, a one-named woman with an accent mark somewhere (I keep forgetting where), a platinum buzz cut and little German glasses, who charged us so much, her bill came in a box. Tim hated all of them. He clearly is not comfortable dealing with fabric-related home decorating choices, but he's not willing to let me have full rein over the windows. His solution was to order wooden slats from Blinds.com and call it a day.

During the actual moving-in process, Tim and I feed off each other in an unhealthy way. It's as if the kids from *Lord of the Flies* were allowed to implement their own corporate relocation. We'll be standing in the new house, waiting for the moving truck to arrive, and Tim will map out our strategy.

"Now, remember. The first thing we do is get the beds ready and the shower curtain hung up. If that's the only thing we get done tonight, it's okay. Because at the end of the day, regardless of what we've accomplished, we're going to want to take showers and hit the sack."

I'm nodding my head vehemently. Yes. We're going to set up the bed, get some nice clean sheets on that bugger, hang the shower curtain. Yes. First thing, that's what we are going to do. We are very adult-like at this point.

Seven hours later, we're cranking Bruce Springsteen, hanging pictures in the kids' rooms and arranging crystal in the dining room china cabinet. We've already alphabetized the spices in the pantry and put the photo albums in chronological order.

Seven hours and three minutes later, we've hit a wall in our energy level and wakefulness, and we are suddenly crawling to the shower, where there is still no shower curtain hung, and to the bed, which is a bare mattress leaning sideways onto a pile of bed frame pieces.

"This is the fifth time we've done this, Diane," Tim says to me as he pulls a sheet of packing paper over him and lies down on the floor. "Next move, we've got to remember to do the hard stuff first."

"Yeah," I say, pulling a dismantled cardboard box over me, "but just think how happy you'll be tomorrow when we can get our hands on the oregano, no problem."

No matter how bad it gets between you and your spouse when you're moving, don't divorce him, and don't kill him. You will have to work hard at resisting the temptation. You may even want to put *not killing* and *not divorcing* your husband on your Moving List. Either of these things could lead to another move, and you don't want that. Plus your black dress is still AWOL.

CHAPTER 12

This Is No Pepsi Commercial

The Joys of Home Ownership

This is awesome. I'm sitting in the living room, just sitting here watching TV. I don't have a paintbrush, a scraper, or a solvent of any kind in my hands. I'm not painting, stripping, varnishing, ripping out, plastering, nailing, or smoothing. We're done with this house.

This is our Youngstown home, a seventy-five-year-old farmhouse that we bought because our tax guy made us. "You're going to pay through the nose next year if you don't buy a house or something," he told us. Can you imagine, two newspaper reporters, barely clearing the poverty level, and the government wants more of our money? They must be jealous.

So we bought this big, old, blue house with a gravel driveway, big detached garage and a big front porch. After eighteen months of working on the house, it's time to move to Cleveland. The house is finished and ready to be put on the market, and with not a minute to spare. Our real estate agent is coming in the morning to look the place over and put up the For Sale sign. I am really enjoying this thing called sitting on the couch in the living room. I have a vague memory of doing this when we were renters.

Then I feel something on my shoulder. And again. And again. Like a drip, drip, drip. I look up and see that it is, indeed, a drip, drip, drip. There is water bowled up in the ceiling directly over my right shoulder. Tim walks into the room, and he looks absolutely naked. It's the first time in a year I'm seeing him without a ladder over his shoulder, power sander in his hand, and a tool belt around his waist.

*"Hey, there's water coming in the ceiling here,"
I tell him, flipping the channel and scooting down
to the next couch cushion.*

*"Alrighty." He turns around and walks up-
stairs, and there is a steady methodical stretch of
activity involving buckets, pipe wrenches, patch,
ceiling paint, and super glue. Okay, now our
house is ready for the market.*

Tip #39: Don't overthink it: some houses are
just plain ugly.

That house in Youngstown turned Tim from a
guy who as a teenager purposefully dripped paint
on his father's Cadillac so that his parents would
never again ask him to help around the house into
a clean-shaven Bob Villa. Eighteen months earlier a potential break in a ceiling dam would have
sent us both into a tizzy. There would have been
wringing of hands, gnashing of teeth, and probably phone calls to 1-800 numbers. Not the case
now.

When we bought that house, it had already
been through a lot. It had been converted into
apartments at one point in its sordid past, large
bedrooms had been divided into two, an exterior

staircase had been installed and uninstalled, and rooms had actually been reduced in square footage by the number of layers of wallpaper and paint on the walls. Tim and I were convinced it was our duty to return this place to its original beauty. Somewhere under layers of wallpaper and paint, there was a charming farmhouse.

Did you know that not all old houses were ever charming? Just because something is old doesn't mean it necessarily was better than the ugliest prefab being built now. Hard to believe, but ugliness was around, even in the early 1900s. We learned that about halfway through our remodeling of that house. We had ripped out a wall upstairs and made two small bedrooms into one large master bedroom. While we were at it, Tim decided to strip the hardwood floor of paint and restore it to the natural wood. Our neighbors across the street watched Tim's progress from operating the loud floor sander at midnight to applying stain and varnish and occasionally leaning out the window to inhale air and exhale retching noises.

Then he decided we needed to restore the wood baseboard trim, ten inches high and looking like it had so much potential. It didn't. Halfway around the room, Tim discovered that sections of the baseboards had been replaced with cheap wood, a definite low point in the house's history.

We thought the wallpaper in the kitchen was the ugliest in the free world until we found what it was covering: bright yellow daisies the size of dinner plates covered green and gold plaid, which covered kettles and apples, which covered a black and red collage of Victorian-time news-papers with drawings of women in big hats and bustles.

"Oh, for crying out loud! Who would put this on a kitchen wall?" Tim yelled in to me. "And speak-ing of which, where *is* the actual wall?!"

Meanwhile I was polishing doorknobs. The doorknobs, too, looked like they held potential. I rubbed an abrasive pasty substance on them every night until the doorknobs were returned to their original silver and my knuckles were returned to the original bone.

"What was I thinking?" I complained to my boss one morning. I had shown up for work with ban-daged hands and a bald spot where I had to cut out a section of my hair that had white primer on it. "I thought this would be fun! I was actually thinking we might enjoy fixing up this house! What the hell was I thinking?"

"You fell for the Pepsi commercial," my city editor, Jack Wollitz, said. He leaned back in his chair, eager to explain his theory. The Jack Wollitz Pepsi Commercial Theory is that when you see the people on the Pepsi commercial fixing up their charming, old house, they're having so much fun that you're convinced that you, too, can have fun like them.

"You'll notice on the Pepsi commercial, the lady is wearing a bandana around her hair, but if you look closely, she's wearing makeup and hairspray," Jack said. "And the paint on her face is strategically placed and kinda foxy. And this couple is laughing—her mouth is actually wide open, if you look at it. It's almost like she's *screaming* with hysterical laughter. Let me ask you this," he leaned forward. "When was the last time you were drinking a Pepsi and laughing while you worked on your house?"

"I used a crushed, empty Mountain Dew can to prop up the ladder," I said. "Does that count?"

I thought about the Jack Wollitz Pepsi Commercial Theory a few weeks later when I found myself in a big nightshirt—and *only* a big nightshirt—frantically ripping out the kitchen floor with my bare hands. The new kitchen floor installers were coming in a matter of minutes, and we hadn't removed the old floor yet. We meant to do this project the night before, but our friend Barry came over, we had a few beers and decided to get up really early the next morning to do it. The more beers we had, the more ridiculously easy the floor-removal project was going to be. By about 1:00 a.m., we were talking about peeling it off with two fingers like a price tag.

The next morning, when I woke up and looked at the clock, I jumped out of bed, gave Tim a push, and we both sprinted downstairs and started gouging and ripping, using whatever screwdrivers, butter knives, and sharp objects we could easily get our hands on. By the time Barry stopped over to pick up Tim for their weekly Saturday morning trip to the hardware store, he saw us both on our hands and knees looking nothing whatsoever like a commercial for any soft drink on this planet. Where's my bandana?

After finally selling the house, we drove back to look at it one day and saw that the yard was dug up like a line of head-to-toe graves. Apparently there had been a sewer line problem, and the new owners were deep in fix-it mode.

"Huh!" Tim said as we cruised by. "The sewer line! That's one thing we didn't have a problem with in that house."

"Speed up," I said, putting on my sunglasses and slouching down. "I think they spotted us."

Tip #40: Appreciate your house's strengths, weaknesses, quirks, and walking dead.

It requires constant gear-shifting, but take your new house and figure out what it is you like about it, and focus on that. Whatever it is, it isn't going to be what you liked about your last house. But try to go with the flow. And start compiling the lessons you've learned.

After our Youngstown home-owning experience, our house in Cleveland was clearly a rebound. It was a neat little thing, contained no wallpaper, needed no improvements, and was completely lacking in character. Still, we were so burned out from Youngstown, we saw the house as one big plus. No basement? Then there's no asbestos, is there? There's no furnace big enough to have its own first name, is there? I think the real reason we chose our house in Cleveland was that it was within walking distance of my sister Kathy's house. And she had The Good Sweeper and a thermometer that worked.

In our townhouse in Virginia, Tim learned the first two lessons in wallpapering: 1) Never Put up Wallpaper with Your Wife, and 2) Never Put up Wallpaper with Your Mother. Wallpapering is a definite negative in any relationship, even one that begins pre-birth.

While wallpapering our bathroom with Tim, I got so angry I kicked the ladder. Not a good idea, when your husband is on that ladder, blathering on about exactly how I should be holding the wet pieces, how I should properly hand him each piece, how I should blah, blah, blah.

For the next room, the powder room, he asked his mother to help him while she was visiting. A cruel trick to play on your mom, who has driven 250 miles, bearing cherry pies and gifts for her grandchildren. If I could have closed the door to shut out the sound of bickering, I would have, but there was no room to swing the door closed. The

two of them, the ladder, and the improperly un-
rolled pieces of wallpaper were completely filling
the room and, according to Tim, my mother-in-
law's elbow movements were the primary source
of the problem.

When we sold the townhouse, we bought my
first dream house back in Ohio. It was a cen-
ter-hall Colonial, very suburban, very soccer
mom. I was thrilled. I felt like I was playing house
where I finally got to be the mom in the JC Penney
catalog. It was brand new, shiny, and beige and
clean. At least until we trashed it. Outside, we had
to put in a lawn but had very little money. We hit
the classifieds and found a guy who would put in
our lawn and landscaping for the equivalent of a
couple good meals. His ineptitude and a record
drought that year turned our new lawn into crispy,
brown weeds. My dream house began to look like
a Burger King that had been shut down for health-
code violations. We soon learned all about fertiliz-
ers, weed-and-feed, Miracle Gro, and sprinklers.

By the time we got to Illinois, we were buying
miniblinds in bulk and wallpapering very few
rooms, choosing instead to paint almost everything in what Tim would call "relo beige." A Swede

wearing khaki could be completely camouflaged in there. That house taught us about heating systems and what happens when it gets really, really cold in Chicago—cold enough for ice to form on the furnace ventilation system on the roof. What happens is the vent freezes shut, and the furnace automatically turns off. The good news is it only happens when it's very cold, below zero, and very late at night, and it happens for a good reason—you won't be asphyxiated in your sleep. However, late at night when it drops below zero and you're freezing your butt off, you start to fantasize about going to sleep on a nice, warm beach for a long, long time.

We had some trouble getting furnace repairmen to get up on our roof. They would show up on triple overtime, and with my offer to slip them an extra $20, would still refuse to get up there.

"It's dark," one guy said to me, seemingly amazed that I didn't know this already. "And I'm guessing slippery, with the ice and all."

Tim and our neighbor Chris tried to get up there, but it was embarrassing. They set up a little stepladder and stood near it, looking up at the roof with their arms crossed and their chests puffed out, every so often nodding and pointing. Occasionally Chris would readjust the ladder. As if they had any intention of climbing onto that roof. We had to call Chris's brother-in-law Tony, who rides motorcycles and has a death wish. He climbed up onto our roof, kicked the ice off the vent with one foot and yelled down, "Yo, you wanna toss up that Coors Lite you promised me?"

The Illinois house was our first and only haunted house. Half the town had heard about The Little Indian Boy who had been seen on the staircase and in one of the bedrooms of the house. We never saw him, but that didn't keep us from listing the house as a "Native American treasure" when we put it on the market.

In south Jersey, we learned that a nice floor plan does not mean that the house is built any better than Caroline's Barbie dream house. Actually, I suspect it took Tim longer to assemble that plastic pink sorority house from December twenty-fourth through January thirtieth than it took for our own house to be built. Tim learned how to replace all the exterior wood trim, including how to build a stair railing, how to repair a skylight with a ripped-up dishtowel, craft glue, and

Silly Putty, and how to replace a shutter back on the third story without falling to your maiming or death. By this time, one bay of our garage was full of manly things, and we could have run a power tool rental business out of there.

In north Jersey, we learned about septic tanks and wells, since we had both. We learned that the guy whose job it is to empty your septic tank of everything you've flushed down your toilet in the past year is both a god and the Devil. Because he'll take it all away, but first he'll tell you all about it. We learned that when you turn on your faucet and water doesn't come out, you instantly get a thirst that forms kidney stones in your body and dehydrates you into a fever. We learned that there is no such color as "beige." When you're trying to paint a room *a nice beige*, the little card will look beige, the brushstroke on the lid will look beige, the paint in the can will look beige. On the wall, it will look yellow. Or gray, or purple. Or, if it's in a boy's room, pink.

In Kentucky, I learned that when your anal-retentive husband has painted just about every vertical surface of every room in seven houses ("plus ceilings," he's yelling in to me as I write this) you're not going to be happy hiring Danny the Painter to take over the painting for you. I learned I'm not the kind of person who can have nonrelatives in my house every day for three weeks, going into various rooms and closing the doors, playing John Michael Montgomery on a boom box. I learned that "two coats" has different meanings to different people.

"Oh, when you said two coats, I didn't know you meant *two* coats!" he said later.

In Florida, I've learned that classy people will be perfectly fine with a tile floor in their formal living room.

We've lived in ranches, townhouses, Colonials, contemporaries, big houses, and small houses. We've had walls made of paneling, plaster, drywall, and stone. Ceilings made of cedar and ceilings with four-inch stalactites that poke your head if you're more than five foot ten. We've had houses with well water, city water, private water company water that tastes great and is cheap, and private water company water that tastes like rotten eggs and is expensive.

We've lived in houses with gas heat, electric heat, and home heating oil at whatever times each of these energy sources was outrageously inflated. I've adjusted to gas ranges and electric ones, toilets that flush slower than molasses and ones that will suck your underwear in if you don't stand far enough away. I've had water that is Redi-hot and faucets that you have to turn on and go make a pot of coffee and a piece of toast before the water gets warm enough to even brush your teeth comfortably.

I've had pop-out Pella windows and old-fashioned windows painted shut with five coats of lead-based paint; windows with built-in micro-miniblinds, lace curtains, velvet drapes, and puffy Papa Smurf valances. Wood floors, linoleum floors made to look like tile, and tile floors made to look like wood. Finished basements that are nicer than the house I grew up in, no basement at all, and cellars where the dog instinctively knows she can go to the bathroom down there and she won't get yelled at.

In some of our houses, garbage was picked up once a week by the same man who's been picking it up for twenty years, and in other houses the garbage and recycling schedule is so complicated you have to download software to decipher it. In some houses, we could feel free to set up lawn chairs and a grill in the driveway, and in other houses, the neighbors gossiped about us if we took a glass of wine to our own front porch.

By now, Tim and I feel we've truly experienced home ownership. We're the only people I know who can watch *The Money Pit* and not crack a smile. It's just not funny. Tim will frown and point to the TV and say, "See, what did I tell you? He should have reinforced that stairway first, and then his wife wouldn't have fallen through it."

Tip #41: Accept your house as it is. It shows respect and will make the breakup a lot easier.

You and your home have a relationship. It will go along with all the cosmetic changes you want to make, as long as you agree to get along with its quirks and personality disorders. Some of our houses were certifiably insane, but I agreed to live with that as long as I could replace the toilet paper dispensers with ones that didn't fall off the walls. One of our basements had a wall that shot blue bolts of static electricity out to your fingers if you stood near it with your hand outstretched after having arrived there without picking your feet up off the carpeting far enough. I tried fixing the problem, calling an electrician, filling our house with gallons of moisture, but to no avail. The house and I eventually came to an agreement: It could continue to zap clueless visitors during the three winter months and we, in turn, were allowed to remove the smell of potpourri from all cabinets and cupboards in the house.

When negotiating an agreement with your house, be careful not to overstep your boundaries. It has plumbing, electricity, and dangerous gases at its disposal, and it's not afraid to use them.

CHAPTER 13

Now Quit Your Whining and Be Adventurous
Getting to Know Your New Surroundings

I can hear tiny French snores from the backseat. Corto, our visiting guest from the South of France is asleep. Thank God. Maybe he won't realize that I am hopelessly lost in New York and putting our lives at risk. This could easily be an international incident.

We are driving around the Bronx and, according to the signs, will soon be either in Harlem or on our way to Riker's Island, neither of which were on the list of all-American sights I had promised our exchange student. I feel good about the fact that we are still moving, but I have no idea in what direction. I keep missing turns to familiar sounding streets, streets with numbers and red, white, and blue shields.

Next to Corto in the back, my three kids aren't asleep, but they aren't commenting at all. This is vintage driving with Mom: it may take thirty minutes to get somewhere, but it could take up to four hours to get home.

Whenever the Fitzpatrick children get in the car, whether it's a vacation or a quick trip into 7-11, they take water, headphones, and flares. I get lost. I tell the kids we're on another adventure, but they're too old for that line, and everyone knows I'm just lost.

"How far away from Philadelphia did you say we live?" Jack asked me once, when I circled around and around in the city—I could see the Ben Franklin Bridge—there it was! Right up there! I could have easily climbed up that embankment and gotten to it, but what about my car? Still, the idea of actually being on the bridge

held some satisfaction for me . . . but no, I fought the urge. Finding vehicular access to the bridge took us two hours to make what should have been a thirty-minute trip.

"Shut up!" I snapped back at Jack. "We're on an adventure, damn it!"

Tip #42: Get your keys, get in that newly licensed car, and start living!

Moving means new places to go, new things to see, new maps, new directions from new gas station attendants from new Third World countries with limited English skills. In short, new adventures.

When you move to a new city, be the brave one, the one who takes the bull by the horns and gives that mother a good shake. Stop talking about what you used to do, the places you loved to go, all the things you miss about your old home. Get in the car and go exploring. Use every errand-running trip to get lost at least once and make a mental note of the things you discover.

Don't fall into that native trap of thinking that since things are so close, you'll go there "someday." I knew people who had lived within ten miles of Philadelphia their entire lives and had never once seen the Liberty Bell. Our neighbors in northern Virginia would drive to the mall at Tyson's Corners but wouldn't drive to the Mall in DC. I used to beg them to get in the car with us. Okay, sure, we'll get lost, it's too crowded, and there is no parking. But isn't that what makes it an adventure?

Don't be surprised when the verbal directions you're given include identifiers like "get on the four-lane" or "turn where the old dairy used to be." In south Jersey there were two roads called Church Street and Church Road, which actually intersected at a busy shopping area. This anomaly did not seem at all strange to the natives. Getting directions to the soccer party from the soccer field would invariably include the phrase, "Get on Church." I would patiently raise my hand and ask, "Church Road or Church Street?" "Church *Road* or Church *Street?*" "*ROAD or STREET!!??*" The answer was usually: "You know, where we had last year's soccer party. Next to the old dairy." Life just isn't made for the new person.

Just about the time I learned good directions to all the cool stuff (and sometimes even some shortcuts) it would be time to move again and I would have to start all over.

I'm a nerd in several different arenas, but by far my nerdiest venue is history. I love nothing more than to go somewhere where something happened worthy of mention in a history book. I love to marvel at the idea that we are standing on the very spot where _____ (fill in the blank with some well known name) did the first _____ (fill in the blank with some historic achievement). Moving has put us in easy driving distance to a boatload of American history lessons. Of course, getting home is not quite as easy, but we eventually get there. My children are such good sports, they have come with me on so many adventures and not just because I've brought up the fact that they'll have to fix their own fluffernutter sandwich for lunch if they stay home.

In northeastern Ohio, we discovered culture, and signed the kids up for the Akron Symphony's Mini Maestros club, where they made drums out of Quaker Oats boxes and string. We went to the ballet, the theater, and the symphony, and we visited the Rock and Roll Hall of Fame in Cleveland. We found maple syrup festivals, community theater, and potteries. You gotta love the Midwest for good, wholesome fun and cheap dishes. When we'd get to a place that offered little in the way of fascinating facts, I'd just make up something. I told the kids that a spot along I-271 in Macedonia was where the last unicorn lived.

In northern Virginia, we discovered the nation's capital and did more walking around that city than I thought was possible. We pushed a stroller to the White House, the Capitol Building, Lincoln Memorial, Vietnam Veterans Memorial, Jefferson Memorial, and Arlington Cemetery. We took picnic lunches to the Mall, marveled at the cherry trees in bloom, posed with life-size cut-outs of George and Barbara Bush, and left a trail of pacifiers through every Smithsonian museum in town. We drove out to Mount Vernon, to Annapolis and several Civil War battle sites. We went as high as the top of the Washington Monument and as low as the caves at Luray Caverns. We cured my fear of bridges, fear of heights, fear of being underground, fear of water, and fear of being shot with a musket, all in one region.

"Hey, just think!" I'd say to the kids at one of the battle sites. "We're standing on the exact spot where someone was bayoneted to death for the Union!"

In Illinois, we often took the train into Chicago, where we discovered museums and zoos, as well as how fast you can get three kids, a stroller, a camera case, and a diaper bag out of the train door before it automatically closes on one of you. Every Christmas we viewed the department store window displays and the big tree in Macy's. We walked along Navy Pier and went to the top of Sears Tower. We drove north and became regulars at the Renaissance Fair in Wisconsin, adding to our medieval phase by also becoming frequent patrons of Medieval Times. These trips added wooden swords, jester hats, and fake nose rings to our collection of totally useless things to save in our basement.

When we lived in south Jersey, we were regulars at the Liberty Bell, Independence Hall, and the Betsy Ross House. We were there so often, I had my favorite tour guides and knew the nuances of each of their talks. We also discovered Washington's Crossing and investigated both the New Jersey and Pennsylvania sides. We marveled at how narrow the river was at the spot where George Washington crossed on Christmas night to attack the British and turn the Revolutionary War. Michael tried to walk across it.

"Hey, you guys!" I would yell to the kids. "I'm standing on the exact spot where George Washington may have stood, maybe, before he got on the boat, in this general vicinity somewhere!"

Princeton also became a favorite place of ours. We would take long walks around the campus, looked at gargoyles on buildings, visited Revolutionary War battle sites, and once put together our own Einstein tour.

"Look, kids!" I yelled from the steps of the Institute for Advanced Study, to the kids, who were slouched in the car with the AC blasting and the radio turned up. "I'm standing on the very steps where Einstein walked every single day to get to work!" Several really smart people looked out their office windows and glared at me.

South Jersey also put us in close proximity to Long Beach Island, where we discovered how beautiful the Jersey shore can be, and Atlantic City, where we learned how tacky and expensive the Jersey shore can be.

When we moved to north Jersey, we discovered New York City—Central Park, the Empire State Building, all the art museums, Ellis Island, and the Statue of Liberty, including one harrowing trip to the crown, where all five of us had our own lives and the lives of all of our immigrant ancestors flash before us. Every summer we saw a Broadway show and bought an egg roll and a contraband purse in Chinatown. We've ridden ferries, subways, trains, buses, and cars into and around the city, saw a Yankees game, and saw a couple of famous people. We toured NBC, walked across the Brooklyn Bridge, and had the best cheesecake in the world.

Driving west, we were in the Poconos and loved to walk through Bushkill Falls to see the waterfalls. Driving north, we were at the ski slopes and the highest elevation in the state.

Once we arrived in Kentucky, we frequented the horse racetrack and the big horse park, marveled at the stately horse farms and the beautiful scenery on every drive everywhere. We experienced horses in every way you possibly can without actually riding one. We went antique shopping in Midway, arts and crafts shopping in Berea, learned the Shaker way at Pleasant Ridge, and toured the Henry Clay estate. We toured three different bourbon distilleries and two wineries. We discovered Red River Gorge, the Daniel Boone National Forest, and Natural Bridge, where I had to stop on our hike to look up at the big rock span and say, "Look, you guys! Can you believe I'm standing on the exact spot where something really big happened to allow this . . . this . . . so how did this happen, do you think?"

"Wind erosion," Jack says flatly. He's sitting on a rock ledge eating a fruit roll-up. "You can go look it up if you want, but everybody learns it in third grade science. It's from wind erosion." This kid is why we never bothered to take a family vacation to any of the great wonders of the world.

In Florida, we've done beaches, lighthouses, beaches, marinas, beaches, inlets, and beaches. We've toured the Everglades on an airboat and a bus with monster truck wheels. We've seen alligators up close and way too personal. We've been to the rustic and beautiful Seminole reservation and to the glitzy and exotic city of Miami. We've compared the beaches of the eastern ocean side to the western gulf side and decided we like the ocean waves but prefer the gulf shells. We've kayaked and canoed on the Loxahatchee River, done enough Disney to last a couple of lifetimes, discovered the Salvatore Dahli museum in

St. Petersburg, and watched a lady make cigars in Ybor City in Tampa.

Soon we'll be moving again, this time to San Francisco. I'm eager to discover the Pacific coast, the San Francisco Bay, buying books at City Lights, riding the cable car, touring vineyards, walking my dog in Golden Gate Park, doing more museums, more nature, more bridges, and more views from more tall buildings. This time my adjustment will be moving from the suburbs to the city, shedding a lot of extraneous possessions, simpler living, and building an empty but vibrant nest.

This country is full of interesting places where you're very unlikely to take a vacation. (Who takes a vacation to New Jersey? Or Cleveland?) Only if you live there can you see what lies beneath. There are adventures right around every corner. You don't need to book a hotel, pack a suitcase, or come within strangling distance of a travel agent in order to experience them. Throw some water bottles and granola bars in the car, along with a flare or two, and be on your way. Soon you'll find yourself standing on the exact spot where someone did something. Send me a postcard.

Made in the USA
Charleston, SC
08 August 2013